Bringing Out the Best in Your Baby

Bringing Out
the Best
in Your Baby

INTRODUCING DISCOVERY PLAY

Art Ulene, M.D.
Steven Shelov, M.D.

Illustrations by Gwen Connelly

Macmillan Publishing Company

New York

•

Macmillan Publishing Company
866 Third Avenue, New York, N.Y. 10022
Collier Macmillan Canada, Inc.

Library of Congress Cataloging-in-Publication Data
Ulene, Art.
Bringing out the best in your baby.
Includes index.
1. Infants. 2. Child development. 3. Educational
games. 4. Child rearing. I. Shelov, Steven P.
II. Title.
HQ774.U44   1986   155.4'18   86-21747
ISBN 0-02-620880-6

10 9 8 7 6 5 4 3 2 1

Book Design by The Sarabande Press

Printed in the United States of America

To Douglas, Valerie and Steven:
each of you "special" in your own unique ways,
each a source of constant joy and light.
—ALU

To my parents; my wife, Marsha;
my children, Joshua, Danielle and Eric;
and all the children I care for.
—SS

Contents

• CONTENTS •

• CONTENTS •

ix

• CONTENTS •

Authors' Note: The information and advice in this book apply equally to babies of both sexes. However, when writing about babies in a book such as this, it is awkward and confusing to constantly shift the gender of pronouns from he *to* she *and* his *to* hers. *We have chosen to handle this problem by using the feminine form of pronouns exclusively when referring to babies. We are sure parents of boys will understand if we depart in this small, but meaningful, way from tradition.*

—ALU

—SS

Foreword

In the beginning, this was to have been a book about using stimulation techniques to make children "special." That idea was quickly abandoned as our consultants reminded us that all children are already special. Our colleagues' advice to us was simple: help parents discover how special their children already are.

Every child is special in some way, but too often we parents fail to recognize these special qualities. Sometimes this happens because we don't know where to look for them, and sometimes it's because we don't make the effort. But every child's unique "specialness" *is* there, waiting to be discovered. The earlier you recognize the special qualities in *your* baby and the more you help her to bring them out, the more special she will be, now and throughout her life.

It's important to point out something that should be obvious: every child is different, so no two children are going to be special in the same way. Society tends, however, to favor and reward certain kinds of "specialness" over others.

For example, we value intellectual and artistic achievement in children more than their human and social qualities. So we brag about the child who reads at the age of two, but overlook the three-year-old who shares her toys. Both are special, but we don't always treat them the same way. We marvel over the four-year-old who plays the violin, but pay little attention to a five-year-old who makes us smile. Both are special: one is lavished with attention and praise, the other is given a pat on the head.

These reactions shape your child's feelings about herself. These are the experiences that determine, at least in part, whether a child will develop high or low levels of self-esteem. To the extent you are able to discover and recognize something—anything—special about your baby, she will begin to feel good about herself. The more she is helped to develop her own special qualities, the more she will have to feel good about for the rest of her life.

We wrote this book to help you do that with your baby. It is based on the scientific knowledge we gained as physicians and on dozens of years of experience as parents. We hope it will be a source of both information and inspiration to you.

But we want to remind you that no book can ever represent the uniqueness of your baby or your family's particular circumstances. There is no substitute for your own intuition and experience. When it comes to *your* baby—*you* are the expert.

—ALU
—SS

Acknowledgments

For steering us (and this book) in the right direction, we thank Lewis Lipsitt, Ph.D.; Richard Aslit, Ph.D.; Frances Horowitz, Ph.D.; Jerome Kagan, Ph.D.; Andrew Meltzoff, Ph.D.; Carolyn Rovee-Collier, Ph.D.; Dorothy Singer, Ph.D.; and Jerome Singer, Ph.D. Their expertise is exceeded only by their love and concern for children.

For unselfishly giving their time and sharing their knowledge with us, we thank Beatrice Beebe, Ph.D.; T. Berry Brazelton, M.D.; William Kessen, Ph.D.; Susan Rose, Ph.D.; Holly Ruff, Ph.D.; Daniel Stern, M.D.; and the staff of the Bank Street School of Education.

For his thoughtful analysis, constructive commentary and gentle encouragement, we thank our editor, Robert Stewart.

For her insightful and incisive commentary on the manuscript and her continual support throughout this project, we thank Nancy Macagno.

For their care, attention and support as this manuscript unfolded, we thank our wives, Marsha Shelov and Priscilla Ulene.

Most of all, we want to acknowledge our gratitude to

and respect for Aimee Liu, without whom there would be no book. She researched tirelessly, wrote beautifully, edited cleverly and made our dream come true.

—ALU
—SS

Bringing Out

the Best

in Your Baby

· I ·

The
Ultimate
Goal

If you had to choose one lifetime gift for your baby, what would it be? A brilliant intellect? A keen sense of humor? Athletic ability? Artistic talent? All of these are laudable goals, but none by itself can assure your child's happiness. There is one inner possession, however, that *is* truly essential for happiness: high self-esteem.

Your most important mission as a parent, in addition to overseeing the physical health and well-being of your baby, is to help her develop the attitudes that nourish high self-esteem:
• *Confidence in the world around her.* Your baby must know that there is some consistency to the world in which she lives if she is to develop self-confidence. This means

1

she must have people around her whom she knows she can trust and a regular schedule of daily activities. A safe physical environment is important, too, so she can explore freely, without fear or injury.

• *A sense of personal power.* Your baby must believe she can make things happen. If she reaches out for a ball and repeatedly finds only thin air, she'll decide after a few tries that it's not worth the effort. If she touches the ball and it rolls across the room, she discovers she can make things *happen!* This discovery tells her there are real rewards for trying, rewards that are within her grasp.

• *Feeling lovable.* Hugging, kissing and talking to your baby provide her with essential information: that she is lovable and loved. This is what she needs to learn the dynamics of love and to discover that she *deserves* to be loved. Through the intimacy that surrounds her during her first months, she experiences the warmth and affection, the feeling of "connectedness," that establishes her sense of self-worth. She learns that love flows in two directions, that she can both give it and receive it. And she discovers that this process is the most rewarding part of being alive.

• *Feeling special.* Nothing helps an adult's self-esteem more than feeling *special,* and your baby is no different. However, her special qualities may be more difficult to recognize. Little babies seem so dependent and incompetent that it's hard to appreciate their extraordinary capabilities. It's also difficult to spot the subtle differences that make each child "special" in her own unique way.

We have written this book to help you discover those qualities that make your baby so unique. The book is based on our belief (and experience) that a baby's special qualities are easier to find when you know what to look for. No book can ever represent accurately the uniqueness of your baby. You'll have to discover that for yourself. In doing so, you'll help your baby establish high levels of self-esteem that will bring her a lifetime of happiness and health. For any parent, that is the ultimate goal.

The Truth

About

Superbabies

Y ou've probably heard the miraculous stories of children who can conduct symphonies, read Greek, speak Japanese, do calculus and recite the encyclopedia by the age of five. If you're like most parents, these tales must have intrigued you at least a little. The idea that a "Superbaby" can be fashioned out of any "ordinary" infant (but remember, no infant is ordinary!) has intrigued child development theorists for centuries. At no other time in history, however, has the notion been carried to such sophisticated and extensive lengths as we are seeing now.

Today's parents are faced with a continual barrage of advertising and promotion, prodding them to take their babies to new intellectual heights. There are books and videotapes for teaching babies to read. There are flash cards for teaching them math. There are seminars for teaching them foreign languages. And there are full-fledged residential programs for parents who are willing to go the distance in order to create a Superbaby.

Some of these programs take advantage of rote memory to fill infants with a vast collection of facts. Almost from birth, these babies are exposed to dots on flash cards (to learn math), large lettered words (to learn how to read) or images of animals, famous faces or objects (to build "encyclopedic knowledge"). Advocates of this process point to six-month-old infants who are able to recognize dozens of images and toddlers who can read in two or three languages.

Critics argue that there are no scientifically controlled studies that document real benefits from this early training. They believe these Superbabies are either naturally gifted children, who would have learned as much if left alone, or babies whose natural disposition lends itself to rote learning. The most cynical detractors suggest that these children have learned to excel academically because they believe it is the only way to please their parents.

At the other end of the Superbaby spectrum are the "infant stimulation" programs, which focus on the sensory side of an infant's experience. Literally from birth, they shower infants with stimuli designed to speed the process of maturation. These children are presented with flashing lights, bright colors and varied sounds to jog their senses. Their legs and arms are manipulated in exercise programs that will, presumably, enhance their balance and coordination.

Advocates claim that this stimulation speeds development. There are scientific studies that show some physiological benefits, including more rapid weight gain and increased alertness, when premature infants receive extra touch and physical stimulation. But critics note with dismay that the studies do not demonstrate long-term benefits, and they express concern about the mechanical—almost impersonal—way the infants are pushed and prodded. This is not the way, these critics say, to raise a "special" child.

Why, then, are these programs so popular? It's hard to know. Some parents genuinely want to do the best for their babies and don't trust themselves to do it alone. Others may be trying to shape their children to a "superior" ideal they themselves never were able to reach.

Still other parents honestly believe that the only way a child will be able to compete in the twenty-first century is by starting serious training in infancy. We think that, in their haste to push their children to the head of tomorrow's class, many of these parents are losing sight of their babies' most valuable qualities.

Some child development experts *agree* with the early learning enthusiasts on just one point: the *capacity* of babies to learn is underestimated by most parents and many educational programs. These experts *disagree* on the timing (some programs advocate reading to the baby while it is still in utero), the emphasis (some babies are placed under inappropriate pressure to perform well) and the rigidity of many programs (some leave little room for individual differences in learning styles and capabilities among babies).

The critics of early learning believe that—ultimately—a child will end up at the same place no matter when you start the process, but they fear that damage can be done if it's begun too early.

In our advice to you—a parent who wants only the best for your child—we are guided primarily by the following deeply held beliefs:

· All babies are unique.
· Childhood is a time for play and exploration.
· Observation and experience form the best basis for learning.
· Fantasy is an essential part of childhood.
· Emotional and social well-being are at least as important as academic, artistic and athletic performance.

HOW THE "SUPERSTARS" ARE RAISED

One way to explore the issue of early training vs. age-appropriate discovery is to examine the childhood experiences of renowned "geniuses" such as Einstein, Copernicus, Haydn, Mozart, Voltaire, Goethe and Leonardo da Vinci. Author Catharine Morris Cox did just that, reviewing case histories of three hundred geniuses to see if she could find the key to their greatness.

In *Genetic Studies of Genius* she reported that, while most of these great thinkers received encouragement from their parents, none began their studies in the cradle. Most of Dr. Cox's subjects received early education, but not until they were at least three years old.

University of Chicago researcher Benjamin Bloom spearheaded a similar survey of 120 young men and women who were considered to be among the top twenty-five American mathematicians, concert pianists, sculptors, neurologists, swimmers and tennis players. He found that none of their parents had set out to produce a prodigy. In fact, most bent over backward to give their children what they considered a "normal," well-rounded childhood, and consciously avoided teaching academic skills to their pre-schoolers.

Searching for distinct patterns in the way these geniuses were raised, Dr. Bloom identified four key points that held true for virtually every one of the genius subjects, cutting across all fields of achievement:

1. *Each child discovered her area of talent through play or recreation.* The early phases of learning were fun-filled and self-initiated. Whether the learning involved math, art, swimming or music, the parent's role was to provide the opportunity and encouragement to explore.

The future mathematicians and scientists, for example, were simply encouraged to be curious about the world at large, to ask questions and search for answers. None of these prodigy academicians received preschool training in academic subjects; six out of the twenty future neurologists were *slow* in learning how to read!

2. *The most important motivating factor in the early lives of these talents was the home environment.* In almost every case, parents stressed the importance of working hard and doing one's best. The parents themselves served as models of determination and achievement. They also provided their children with environments rich in learning opportunities that reflected their own personal interests.

Parents who played tennis took their infants along with them to the courts. Parents who loved music often had a piano in their house to which their babies had free access.

Parents interested in art took their children with them to museums and galleries. In the homes of all the subjects, but especially the future mathematicians and scientists, parents showed great respect for curiosity and questions and encouraged independent thinking.

3. *Once the child expressed a specific interest or demonstrated ability in a particular activity or field, the parents accepted that direction as the child's priority.* Swimmers, for example, were encouraged to spend extra time at the pool, even if it meant skipping their piano lessons. For future concert pianists, music lessons came first. Homework, playtime and physical exercise were fitted around their practice schedule. But this focusing process usually didn't occur until the children had had several years to develop their interest and talent. Athletes and pianists began taking lessons in earnest around the age of six or seven, but the scientists, mathematicians and artists didn't receive formal training until much later in childhood.

4. *In every case, the families and teachers of these children were essential to their ultimate success.* Early in life, the families' most important contribution was to encourage free exploration and to provide experience that inspired their children's interest in specific fields. As talent emerged, the families' most important job was to find teachers who could meet the children's needs at each stage of development.

The first stage required teachers who made learning fun for the children while teaching basic skills. Later, the children had teachers who served more as mentors, helping them fine-tune the unique abilities that would help them stand out among top competition.

There is no magic program you can use in infancy to

guarantee that your child will become a genius, a star athlete, a captain of industry or a best-selling author. Even if there were, it would be wrong for you to impose such a program on your infant. Your infant is one-of-a-kind. She was born with her own unique set of special qualities, and she needs the freedom and encouragement to develop them. We'll show you how to do that with a process called *Discovery Play*.

· III ·

Discovery

Play

You can program a computer to behave in predictable ways and produce desired results. Human beings (including babies) don't work that way. We need the thrill of discovery to keep us learning. We absorb more knowledge when we are interested in a subject than when we're force-fed information. Beginning in infancy, we learn through trial and error, by observing and testing.

"Childish" play is actually very sophisticated experimentation; the world is your baby's learning laboratory. If left alone, her trials and observations will tend to follow her unique interests and abilities, and she'll discover what she likes and does best.

There is a way to ensure that your baby discovers her own special qualities and true potential. It's a method based on the conviction that children are more than empty memory banks, to be filled on demand. It's a process developed in the belief that parents have more to give their children than flash cards and flashing lights. We call it Discovery Play.

The purpose of Discovery Play is to help parents discover the wonder of their babies as their babies discover the wonder of life. The goal of Discovery Play is high self-esteem for both parents and children.

The key phases of Discovery Play are:

- education (for the parent)
- opportunity (for the infant)
- permission (for the infant)
- natural reinforcement (by both, for both)

Education

The educational phase of Discovery Play is designed to make you more capable of recognizing your baby's developmental potential and progress. It's easier to bring out the best in your baby if you are aware of the many talents that are present, but which often go unrecognized. For example, did you know that:

- Within minutes of birth your baby is able to imitate facial expressions of the people around her.
- Your newborn prefers your voice to a stranger's.
- Several days after birth your baby can identify you by smell.
- Your infant prefers specific images and patterns and, as her color vision develops, certain colors as well.
- Months before she utters her first word your baby understands much of what you say to her.

The educational part of Discovery Play is also designed to inform you of your infant's limitations. Understanding that your baby is not physically or physiologically capable of certain tasks at certain ages makes you less likely to present her with impossible challenges that can lead only to frustration. Why expect a month-old baby to distinguish between colors if color vision doesn't mature until two to three months? Why get upset when your six-month-old can't find a ball under a blanket if children this age believe that objects cease to exist when they move out of sight?

We hope this book will teach you what babies, in general, can and cannot do. We'll show you how to recognize where your baby is following the norms and where she is exceptional. You'll learn many things you can do to help your child demonstrate her own unique qualities and to bring out the best of her special talents.

Opportunity

Your role as a parent involved in Discovery Play is to create opportunities for your baby to demonstrate her unique brand of "specialness." That's not as tall an order as it may sound. Most babies are born with a determination to prove themselves. If you give your baby plenty of room to express herself, she'll use every inch. There are several things you can do to ensure that she gets the maximum opportunity:

• *Provide a responsive environment.* There's only one way for your baby to learn that she can make things happen in her world: she must see them happen. A nursery filled with toys that *you* wind up may prompt a fleeting smile, but your baby won't get any lasting benefits from them. She needs access to objects that respond to *her* movements, wheels that *she* can turn, balls that *she* can bounce, paper that *she* can tear. Your baby needs toys and objects that she can manipulate in several different ways. These help her discover that she has choices and that each choice she makes has a unique consequence.

• *Balance your baby's success and failure rates.* Many parents are so eager to see their infant succeed that they never let the baby fail. At the slightest sign of frustration, they move a toy closer so the baby can reach it. If the baby has difficulty turning the crank on her jack-in-the-box, Dad jumps in and turns it for her. As a result, the infant never gets a chance to stretch and push herself. She never achieves the satisfaction of conquering a real challenge.

You can balance your baby's success rate by creating a setting that offers her different types of challenges geared to her age and abilities. Let her choose her own targets. She'll naturally be attracted to those which are neither too hard nor too easy. Your job is to monitor the baby's activity, but not interfere unless she becomes distraught. A little grunting is to be expected if your baby is exerting herself; crying is a sign she needs your help.

• *Send positive messages.* By showing your baby that you share the excitement of her accomplishments, you enhance her own delight in her achievements. The messages are not necessarily verbal. You can open your eyes and mouth wide to show how thrilled you are when your baby shakes her rattle. You might nod your head in time with her arm and leg movements, or produce sound effects (*"Kaaabam!"*) to match the beat of her toy hammer.

Most parents do this unconsciously as they watch their

children play. Child development experts call this process "attunement." Studies of parent-child interaction show that these shared moments occur approximately once every sixty-five seconds in an average play period.

• *Encourage communication.* Establishing two-way communication early lets your baby know you want her to express herself and play an active part in the world around her. You also show her that what she thinks and feels is important to you. Use as many different kinds of communication as you can. Talking, reading and singing to your baby are wonderful ways to establish contact, but touching, looking and listening are also important. (Yes, listening is a form of communication; it tells your baby you want to hear what she has to say.)

If you listen carefully you'll hear distinct combinations of sounds that resemble words and sentences. And you'll begin to read the subtle nuances of your baby's unique expressions which reveal her feelings and moods.

• *Cultivate respect.* An essential ingredient of any relationship is mutual respect. Your relationship with your baby is no exception. It may be difficult to generate something as complicated as respect for an infant who spends most of her time sleeping and eating, but just look at life from your baby's perspective. She must learn to regulate her own body after nine months of complete dependency inside the uterus. She has to contend with changing sensory capabilities that make the world appear different from one day to the next.

She is learning to identify with you and other members of the family while discovering that she is a separate individual in her own right. She is beginning to learn the basic physical properties of the world around her—a world as foreign to her as Mars would be to any of us. That's a lot of information for one tiny baby to assimilate, but your baby does it, and for that she certainly deserves your respect.

What about her respect for you? That too develops from birth as you establish the give-and-take within your relationship. There's no reason to accept mistreatment from your baby (hair pulling, tantrums, biting, etc.). Standing up for your health and sanity does not mean that you love your baby any less. In fact, the consistent limits you set will help her establish a secure understanding of her universe.

Permission

Permission is a critical element of Discovery Play. Your baby will never get a chance to develop her special qualities unless she is allowed to experiment and explore. She needs the freedom to explore within safe limits without your hovering anxiously over her shoulder. (You probably never thought of your anxiety level as a restraint on your child's development, but it can be.) She needs permission to express any thought on her mind without having to worry about a judgmental comment or reprisal. She needs permission to disagree with you or be different from you without risking the loss of your affection.

To an adult, these statements might sound silly. Just because you disagree with your baby doesn't mean you care for her any less. You know that and we know that, but your three-month-old may not. So you'll have to prove it to her with unqualified acceptance and love, even in the face of conflict.

Natural Reinforcement

At the risk of attaching too much importance to every breath you take around your baby, we'd like to point out that every action by one human around another causes some sort of reaction. It's especially true with babies and parents, although parents are often unaware that it's happening since their babies' responses are subtle and fleeting. Nonetheless, studies of babies tell us that even our most insignificant actions can have a very real impact on our children.

As an adult you can tell the difference between important and unimportant events. Your baby doesn't have that reasoning power yet, so she may attach more importance to some of your actions than is justified. You can't read your baby's mind, but you can make some intelligent guesses about what she's thinking by paying careful attention to her actions and expressions.

An important part of Discovery Play is recognizing how "connected" you and your baby are and putting that fact to work. Pay close attention to your baby's actions and expressions, and you'll naturally start sending more meaningful reactions and expressions back to her. She'll be less likely to misinterpret you and you'll be more likely to send her positive "reinforcement" messages. By reinforcement we mean natural things like kissing, cuddling, rocking, stroking, smiling and laughing. These shared moments are guaranteed to make you and your child feel good about yourselves and each other.

D I S C O V E R Y   P L A Y

Discovery Play at Work

Soon after they brought Stephanie home from the hospital, her parents began reading and singing to her from books with large, bold pictures. Her parents discovered that Stephanie's interest remained high as long as they held the pages fairly close to her face. As Stephanie grew older, she discovered she could reach out and touch the pictures. That's when her parents started to create their own books, using materials of different textures to make the game even more interesting for Stephanie.

When Stephanie was about eight weeks old, her parents taught her how to control the brightly colored mobile that hung above her crib. They would attach one end of a satin ribbon to the arm of the mobile and the other end to one of the baby's ankles. She quickly discovered that she could make the little figures dance and spin by kicking her leg. Her parents discovered Stephanie's ability to solve problems the first time they moved the ribbon to her other leg. In five minutes, she had figured out exactly which new muscles she had to work to bring the mobile back to life again.

By the time she was three months old, Stephanie's parents were taking her on special outings each week. Sometimes they would visit museums. She would stare intently at the large, brightly colored paintings and lifelike sculptures. Her parents discovered that Stephanie's range of vision was essentially the same as theirs. Stephanie discovered that the world was not just black and white. She liked red and blue the best.

Stephanie and her dad began playing peekaboo together when she was just four months old. Over the next year she eagerly experimented with all possible variations of this game. Stephanie discovered that her father really wasn't gone just because she couldn't see him.

When Stephanie was a year old, her favorite games involved plastic containers which she filled with small objects or water, then emptied. In the kitchen her mother set up a special shelf with Stephanie's equipment so she could help "cook" while dinner was being prepared each evening. Stephanie discovered *that some things were smaller than others, and she soon learned the meaning of "in" and "on" and "under." Her mother discovered Stephanie's artistic talents, as her daughter tirelessly fingerpainted on the counter with chocolate sauce.*

By the time Stephanie was two, she was talking a mile a minute. She knew several of her favorite books by heart and had "written" books of her own using crayons and fingerpaints. At the zoo she was especially fond of the elephant and the baby camel. When the family went on a stroll at the nearby shopping mall, Stephanie insisted on saying hello to several of the shopkeepers with whom she'd become friends. Her curiosity was insatiable—and often exhausting for her parents. But it was all worth it when they saw the delight in Stephanie's eyes as she announced her latest discovery or achievement.

Discovery Play is a partnership process between parents and children. It increases the opportunities for a child to express herself. It enhances her efforts to learn about the world around her. It provides her with experiences that make her feel special and promote high levels of self-esteem.

You, too, will feel the benefits of Discovery Play. You'll get to know your child intimately and honestly. You'll discover your child's likes and dislikes, her strengths and weaknesses. You'll discover characteristics and capabilities that you might otherwise miss. You'll come to understand her temperament, and you'll probably respond to her moods more appropriately. You'll learn how much stimulation is right for your baby, and how much is too much. Most important, you'll enjoy your baby more. The closeness you can achieve through Discovery Play will enhance your respect and love for your baby, establishing a secure foundation for the future of your relationship.

The concept does not stop with the end of infancy. As time passes, you'll broaden the scope of your activities together. You and your baby will be equal partners in play as she becomes more active and establishes more control over her body. Before long, her mastery of speech will open up new, and sometimes more challenging, ways to communicate with each other.

In time, you'll find yourself adjusting almost unconsciously to your baby's mood and she to yours, slowing down or speeding up to get in tune with each other's activity levels and emotional states. Sometimes you'll boost her spirits, and at other times she'll boost yours. As you interact, you'll mutually pull the relationship into balance, bringing out the best in each other.

As her parents, you are the most influential people in your baby's life. She depends on you to help her learn that she is both lovable and capable of loving. It's up to you to expose her through play to all the ways she can influence the world around her. Only you can help her establish the security, confidence and self-esteem she needs to try things that are beyond her immediate reach, but which she can achieve with a little work.

Bit by bit, she'll discover for herself what success is all about and what she likes and does best. She'll develop her own appetite for achievement and risk-taking, her own style of learning and problem-solving. By nourishing this excitement and determination, you'll lay the best possible foundation for her future. Through these simple activities early in life, your baby establishes the basic confidence, independence, curiosity, energy and sense of self to meet the world on her own terms.

· IV ·

Rules

of the

Game

As you get to know your new baby you'll soon discover she is learning all the time. What you may view as everyday routine, she sees as a great adventure. What you consider work, she accepts as play: your infant cannot wait to explore new situations and problems.

For her, learning and play are the same thing. Each new discovery she makes, each new skill she acquires—no matter how small—is a source of great pleasure to her. Collectively, these accomplishments are the building blocks of your baby's self-confidence and self-esteem.

Bringing out your baby's appetite for learning is one of your most important jobs as a parent, although the task can be a bit intimidating. Especially if you're a first-time parent, it's easy to feel overwhelmed by the sudden responsibility for your child's care and well-being, and you may feel unprepared to serve as her teacher as well. It might help to remember that you're *both* going to be learning a lot during your first years together. In this sense, you're more of a partner than a teacher.

CREATING COMFORTABLE ROLES FOR YOURSELF AND YOUR BABY

In general, the best advice we can give you is to relax and enjoy your baby. But there may be times when that isn't enough: when she's cranky or struggling to learn something difficult or when the two of you are simply not attuned to each other. At these times, it may help to review the following suggestions:

1. *Let your baby take the lead.* Infants have their own schedules for learning and exploring. If you make the proper resources available and provide appropriate encouragement, your child will learn at a rate that is comfortable for her. If you push her to learn something before she is interested, you may create frustration and resentment that will retard her development in the long run.

Instead, look for areas that naturally interest your baby. Then make it easy for her to make her own discoveries in these areas. The joy of learning this way will have a far more lasting positive effect than any rote learning she performs in these early months.

2. *Show your baby that she is smart and capable.* Even though she is born with the ability and eagerness to learn, it's all too easy to convince her that she is *not* bright and that she *cannot* succeed. This happens automatically if she

is continually presented with tasks she cannot do and challenges she cannot meet. It happens when too much emphasis is placed on her learning performance. A simple frown on your face may be taken as a rejection. A long silence after she makes the wrong response may cause her to question the wisdom of attempting any response in the future.

You can reduce the chance that your baby will suffer this problem by structuring more opportunities for success. Present her with problems you know she can solve as well as tasks that push her limits.

Praise her accomplishments, but give her unqualified love and acceptance when she fails. Let her know that you value her attempts. Building your baby's self-confidence this way will encourage her to develop herself to the best of her abilities.

3. Develop your own zest for learning. To your baby, learning is play and all things are possible. She is born with a love for learning, and it's up to you to preserve it. So try to look at the world through her eyes, viewing everything as an entirely novel and challenging experience.

Ask yourself the questions that she must be asking, then look for the answers with her. You may be surprised how much you'll discover yourself when you open up this way.

4. Step back to your own childhood. You won't be able to remember how you felt as an infant, but you probably have lots of memories of early childhood. Take these reflections into account as you begin to establish your relationship with your own baby. This perspective will help you better understand your baby's needs and feelings and may keep you from becoming impatient with your infant.

5. Make special time available. Your baby deserves your

undivided attention for at least *some* time each day. The amount of time you can set aside will depend on your other responsibilities, but you shouldn't use a busy schedule as an excuse to miss a day. Your baby needs to be the sole focus of your attention at least once a day. Frankly, you need it, too. This is the time when each of you will let the other know that nothing in life is more important to you.

At today's frantic pace, with pressures from work, finances and adult relationships, it may be difficult to find the amount of time you think is adequate for these special sessions with your baby. You'll be tempted to skip some days until you have a whole afternoon or evening to spend with her.

Do not make that mistake. You can never bring these precious days back, so don't allow a single one to go by without spending some focused time with your child, even if it's only fifteen minutes.

CREATING THE RIGHT ENVIRONMENT FOR LEARNING

Contrary to what many toy companies would have you believe, there is no perfect toy or piece of equipment that will make your baby smarter or happier than other children. Your infant learns from everything in her environment, including people, household objects, noises, lights, smells and tastes. A nursery filled with the world's most expensive toys won't provide your child with as much positive stimulation as a kitchen or backyard stocked with everyday household objects.

Child development experts have been studying the relationship between the environment and early learning to find out if certain combinations of stimuli are especially beneficial. Their research shows that there is a very definite link between environment and early development. The following guidelines for designing your child's living environment are based on the results of these studies:

1. Create a *responsive* environment. Stay away from toys or objects that you must operate for your baby. Balls, blocks, rattles, stacking dishes, patterned cloths or paper that can fold or tear will appeal far more to your child *over the long run* than a windup bear that walks and talks.

A mobile she can manipulate herself is more educational and a hundred times more interesting than a mobile she can see but not control. For safety's sake, you'll need to supervise many of these activities closely, but the special learning benefits to your baby make them well worth the extra caution and attention on your part.

2. Create a *human* environment. Your baby learns more from the people around her than from any toys or objects. Include her in as many activities as possible. Encourage her siblings, relatives and neighbors to play and talk with her. Take her out of the house to the park and on errands so she gets used to seeing strangers.

3. *Vary* the environment. Babies respond to novel stimuli. Take advantage of this by rotating the available toys in your child's nursery. Change the elements in her mobile frequently. Put up new posters or pictures in her room every few weeks. Gather a large collection of books and read a different one to her each day. Expose your baby to as many different sensations as possible.

4. Tailor the environment to your baby's *individual interests*. She may be more interested in objects than people,

or vice versa. She may spend more time examining things closely than trying to manipulate them. Take advantage of her natural inclinations by giving her the tools she needs to build on them.

If she lights up around people, don't shut her in a room by herself with games and puzzles. If she is most fascinated by objects, don't spend all day trying to get her to play with other children. Keep her routine balanced and varied, but if she has a natural bent, bring it out.

5. Use the *whole* environment. Take advantage of time together during changings and feedings to talk to your baby and teach her about the world around her. Look for learning and play tools for her wherever you go. These may include interestingly shaped foods and brightly colored boxes at the grocery store or a large shell at the seashore. (Be sure that anything you do give your baby is clean and safe for her to put in her mouth.)

Teach your child that the whole world is filled with interesting things to explore and discover. Make her aware that learning is a full-time opportunity.

6. Encourage *exploration*. Give your baby as much freedom as possible to move around her environment. Once she starts to crawl and then to walk, you may have to block her access to hazardous areas, such as hot tubs, pools, workshops and under kitchen sinks, but every other area of your home and yard should be made as childproof as possible and then opened up to her.

As your baby gets old enough to learn some facts about safety, make sure they are learned well. In the long run, your baby will be safer if she learns to take care of herself than if she relies entirely on you for protection.

7. Establish a regular *routine*. While it's important to vary the individual stimuli in your baby's world, it is also important to set up a secure structure overall. This means working out a daily schedule for eating, sleeping, going for walks. It will probably take several months to establish these patterns after your baby is born, and there are bound to be exceptions when she is ill or teething, but both you and your baby will be happier once the routine is established.

GOOD LEARNING PRACTICES

These guidelines for Discovery Play will help you and your baby learn more about each other and life in general. They will also make your time together more joyful.

1. *Listen to your child's signals.* Try to engage your child in Discovery Play only when she is awake, alert and relaxed. Don't set a fixed time for "learning" each day unless you discover that your child has a regular time when she is especially receptive to new information.

Remember that your ultimate objective is to make learning an enjoyable, positive experience. You can't achieve this by pushing her to learn when she's sick, cranky or tired.

2. *Rotate activities for different skills.* Give your child a varied menu of play that stimulates all aspects of her development. At first you'll want to concentrate on activities that stimulate your infant's developing sensory system. After a month or so you'll begin adding games that encourage motor and cognitive development.

Don't establish a rigid routine, but do try to include several different types of games in each of your play sessions. Let your child's interests guide the final selections and don't be offended if she rejects your favorite choices.

3. *Use the shortest, clearest explanations possible.* Long before your child learns to talk herself she will be able to understand what you say. Be sure to tell her what you're doing and why. Explain what happens when she pushes her ball or shakes her rattle. If you give her rules, tell her why it's important to follow them. When you talk to her, use clear, simple language, not baby talk. Let her know that you respect her intelligence.

4. *Don't "drill" information.* When you and your baby are exploring a new concept or word together, look for as many different ways to approach the information as you can. Repetitious information quickly bores and confuses children, because they assume the concept is limited to that single example. Remember, your aim is to keep learning fun and challenging for both you and your child.

5. *Quit while the interest is high.* It's very tempting to keep reading or playing with blocks for hours when your baby is having a good time, but you should quit while you're ahead. If you notice any signs of fatigue or distraction, stop immediately. Waiting until your baby is out of sorts can make it difficult to engage her in Discovery Play the next day.

Young children tend to pick up a continuing activity or experience exactly where they last left off. If your child ends one session in a bad mood, she'll remember that bad mood when you try to start the next session. Avoid the negative association by ending every session on a positive note.

SMOOTHING THE WATERS

The reality of childrearing is more demanding and less controllable than most people imagine. No matter how much you want to be the calm, confident parent, there are bound to be times when trouble arises. Tempers flare. Fatigue strikes. Catastrophes occur. Expect it.

Try not to overreact. Count to ten. Take a deep breath. Cry. Ask someone for help. But whatever you do, don't take it out on your baby. She won't understand what you're saying or doing, and it won't solve any problems. Lashing out at your baby will only leave you feeling extremely guilt-ridden afterward.

You may be able to avoid some of these crises by setting up a fairly regular routine that both of you follow. Gradually, your baby will learn the pattern and begin to conform to it. She'll discover there's a particular time each day to take a nap, to eat and to bathe. Knowing when these events will occur allows her to prepare for them emotionally ahead of time. Even if she fights going to sleep or hates taking a bath, it helps her to accept these rituals if she knows when they're going to happen.

By the same token, the more predictable your moods and behavior are, the more content your baby will be. This doesn't mean you must always be a saint for your baby's sake. Quite the contrary. Your baby needs to learn that people have many different moods and specific reactions to particular kinds of emotional situations.

But, for this information to make sense to her, there must be some consistency and predictability to your behavior. She needs to see the cause as well as the effect. If you are upset when you walk in the door after a frantic day at the office, your baby has no way of knowing that your anger is not directed at her.

Of course, not all of your moods are going to have rational explanations. Neither will your baby's. There will be days when you feel exhausted for no apparent reason. Your baby will have days when she is cranky without explanation.

Protect yourself and your baby when your moods are out of sync by planning low-key activities that will minimize stress. Be prepared to abandon your scheduled plans. Instead of running errands or gearing up for a trip to the park, stick to calm, gentle activities. These quiet times may help you both.

As you and your baby become acquainted and begin exploring your world together, the most important thing you can do is remain flexible. No doubt your infant will learn some skills sooner than you expect, and others later. She may be exuberant and full of action for five days in a row, then retreat for three. She's bound to go through many ups and downs in what may seem, to you, a chaotic pattern.

If you push her to perform on your schedule or at your level of enthusiasm, you'll both become needlessly frustrated and irritated with each other. Instead, stay as relaxed as you can. Let your baby know that you love her and value her no matter what her mood or behavior.

· V ·

The Brain

and the

Senses

Although we date a person's age from the moment of birth, there is evidence that babies actually begin to think and feel during the final weeks of pregnancy. The fetus at this point has the physical equipment needed to function on its own and begins to test that equipment in much the same way it will after birth.

Only recently have researchers begun to explore the mysteries of fetal learning. Their purpose is to better understand the special developmental problems of premature infants and to enhance the quality of early education. In the process, they have come up with some astonishing findings that may help you better understand your baby.

At the University of North Carolina at Greensboro, psychologist Anthony De Casper is investigating the ability of newborns to recognize the sounds, voices and information they heard during the final weeks of pregnancy. De Casper created an experiment in which babies less than two days old could "tell" him which sounds they preferred to hear.

In each baby's mouth he placed a nipple that was attached to an audiocassette player. If the baby sucked in a particular pattern of long and short bursts, she would hear one tape. If she sucked in a different pattern, she would hear a second tape. Even the tiniest newborns quickly learned this system and were able to bring on the sounds they preferred by sucking in the necessary manner. These studies revealed that babies preferred sounds with which they had become familiar before birth.

The first of De Casper's studies pitted the mother's voice against a strange woman's voice. The babies adjusted their sucking patterns so they could hear their mothers' voices. Another experiment offered the baby a choice of the father's voice or the sound of the mother's heartbeat (as it would have sounded to the baby in utero). The babies' sucking indicated a preference for the sound of the more familiar heartbeat.

Finally, De Casper asked sixteen pregnant women to read aloud the book *The Cat in the Hat* twice a day for the last six and one-half weeks of pregnancy, thereby exposing their babies to this story for about five hours by the time they were born. Shortly after birth, the babies were given the sucking test. On one tape they heard their mothers' voices reading *The Cat in the Hat;* on the other, the mothers read another children's poem. The babies consistently preferred *The Cat in the Hat.*

We've met several new parents who tried similar experiments on their own. One father sang a cowboy song to his unborn baby each night during the end of his wife's pregnancy. After the infant was born she would quiet and smile whenever her father sang that song, but no other. Many mothers have stated that their newborn babies seemed to prefer the same type of jazz or classical music that played regularly in their homes during late pregnancy.

Researchers like De Casper are challenging the old assumptions that all newborn responses to stimulation are reflexive, that the baby reacts automatically. It is true that a newborn predictably will grasp anything placed in her hand. She'll suck any object put in her mouth. She'll pull her foot back if it is pricked and blink when a light is flashed in her eyes. Pediatricians look for these reflexes immediately after birth to make sure that the baby is normal. But not all reflexive movements are so straightforward. Some are so subtle—or complex—that they look intentional:

· Whenever your newborn's head falls suddenly backward or to the side, or she is raised or lowered abruptly, she'll perform what's called the Moro reflex. Her arms will shoot out and back. Her mouth will open and close. To you, she looks as if she's panic-stricken, but she will regain her composure within moments once she achieves a comfortable position.
· Touch your baby's cheek and she'll turn toward your finger, as if consciously searching for the source of stimulation. This is called the Babkin or rooting reflex. Psychologists claim it is one of many reflexes that evolved to help the human baby find food and protection during the first days of life.

· Gently tap the bridge of your baby's nose or clap your hands within eighteen inches of her head and she'll shut her eyes tightly, as if telling you to stop.
· Hold your infant, stomach down, in midair. Her legs will push out and she'll try to lift her head, making her look as though she's flying.

While all babies normally have these basic reflexes at birth, they quickly begin to modify their movements. Researchers have found that infants less than two days old can vary the intensity of their sucking depending on the specific circumstances. The babies suck heartily if their bottles contain sugar water, but slow almost to a standstill if it is changed to plain water or the bottles are empty.

The softer the nipple, the warmer and quieter the room, the harder a baby will suck. As she becomes full, her sucking slows down. This is just one example of how babies learn early to adapt their reflexes to their individual needs and preferences.

As your baby matures and develops the neurological control to direct her larger movements consciously, some of her reflexes will begin to fade. Her behavior will become increasingly intentional, reflecting her unique temperament and personality. Everyone in the family will start to notice little things your baby does differently from other babies. You may begin to talk about her general disposition as "calm," "bouncy," "happy" or "super energetic." Many of these distinctive characteristics will last throughout her infancy. Some will endure her entire life.

Your child's personality is reflected not only in the particular things she does, but also the pattern in which she organizes her activities. She may be very energetic in the morning, for example, when the rest of the family is out of the house, but very quiet and observant in the afternoon or evenings when everyone is home.

Some babies seem to spend all their waking hours in vigorous physical activity, while others are downright placid. Some sleep long and deeply, while others seem only to toss and turn. In fact, every baby has the same basic moods, which psychologists call "states," even though each child balances them differently.

British pediatrician Peter Wolff pinpointed seven states that your infant will move through every day:

State 1   Regular sleep or deep sleep, when the baby is still, pale and breathing evenly

State 2   Irregular sleep, when the child jerks, startles and breathes irregularly

State 3   Periodic sleep, alternating bursts of deep and irregular sleep

State 4   Drowsiness, when the infant's eyes begin to droop, giving them a glazed look, and breathing begins to slow in preparation for sleep

State 5   Alert inactivity, when the child's body is still, but she looks eagerly at her surroundings; breathing is rapid and irregular (this is the state when a baby is most receptive to learning)

State 6   Waking activity, marked by spurts of physical activity with lots of twisting and stretching, but without a great deal of visual focus

State 7 Crying, which needs little explanation except to point out that whimpering and mur-
muring are *not* the same as cries, which
involve a great deal of movement, flushing
of the skin, wailing and, later in infancy,
tears

Each baby establishes her own cycle of states very early
in life. For the most part, this pattern remains constant
regardless of the noise and activity going on around her.
Although you often can calm a crying baby by holding,
lifting, rocking and/or stroking her, nothing you can do
will change the overall balance of her states because it is
part of her own special makeup.

Because these states have a critical effect on your child's
ability to learn and explore her environment, it's important
that you take them into account when planning her activities. If, for example, your baby is usually alert and quiet
(State 5) right after eating, this is the best time to read to
her because it's the time when she'll be most interested in
looking and listening.

If she tends to wake up in the morning with a lot of
physical energy (State 6), this is the time to give her free
rein to move and stretch.

If she tends to become drowsy (State 4) in the middle
of dinnertime, your best bet may be to move her dinnertime up an hour so that you can put her to bed earlier.
The best time to put your baby down to sleep is just as
she's starting to show signs of weariness. Don't let her get
overtired. Once she passes a certain stage of fatigue, she'll
begin to fight sleep and it will become harder to get her to
bed.

Becoming familiar with the normal pattern of your baby's states will also help you determine when she is having an "off day." If she is crying more than usual, it may be a signal she is cutting a tooth, coming down with a cold or simply feeling cranky. As you become more sensitive to her personal signals, you'll learn to distinguish her bad mood cries from cries of hunger or pain, and you'll develop strategies for consoling her.

There is mounting evidence that abnormal state patterns can also signal more serious conditions. At Brown University, Dr. Barry Lester's research indicates that babies who have an extremely high-pitched and inconsolable wail may in fact be suffering from neurological or other disorders. While this research is still inconclusive, it points out the importance of parents "tuning in" to their babies early in life.

PERCEPTION AND LEARNING

Your baby's ability to learn is governed by the development of her sensory system. She will form her perception of the world around her on the basis of what she sees, hears, feels, smells and tastes. Despite the remarkable sensory development that has taken place in utero, your newborn baby's sensory system still has many limitations compared to yours. Slowly but surely, these restrictions will disappear as her nervous system matures.

Many psychologists suggest that the gradual unfolding of the senses helps protect babies from being swamped by stimuli. If babies were able to see the world as adults do, they probably would be overwhelmed by it. Thanks to her physiological makeup, your infant comes into a world that appears to her quite manageable. For example:

· Your newborn baby can focus only on objects approximately ten inches away, and she can make out only relatively large objects or features. You are within your infant's range of focus whenever you hold or feed her, and your most expressive features, your eyes and mouth, are large and distinctive enough that your baby sees them clearly even at birth. This may be why babies show a clear preference for faces over other patterns from the first hours of life.

· Although babies have extremely limited motor skills at birth, their sense of touch is well developed, and they will reach out randomly to objects and textures within that same ten-inch range. This means they touch only those things that are within their visual field, and they can see only those things that are within their reach. In this way, their visual limitations actually help them discover that seeing and touching are two ways to explore the same object.

One key reason why infants vary in their rates of intellectual development is that each sense develops at its own rate and at different rates in different infants. For example, your baby's hearing may be unusually acute at birth while her vision develops relatively slowly. Discovery Play will help you to recognize your child's capabilities in each sensory area.

CONNECTING THE SENSES

Infants learn best when they receive information via just one sense at a time, unlike older children and adults, who learn by exploring the world with all senses simultaneously. Getting too much sensory input may leave your infant with a different impression than you would have of the same event.

For example, if your three-month-old sees a toy moving across the room, she will recognize it when she later sees it standing still. But if the toy made a noise the first time she saw it, she might not recognize it later without the accompanying sound. A six-month-old will easily remember a doll she has played with previously, but may not recognize it if she is only allowed to look at it a second time and not to play with it.

The process of linking information from several different senses to create a single image is what psychologists call "cross-modal matching." This ability allows us to anticipate how an object will feel or sound simply by looking at it. By the same token, we can envision how an object will look by running our hands blindly over it.

Adults use this skill constantly. For example, while touch-typing, the feel of the keyboard translates to mental images of the letters on the keys. When people read lips, the visual image of a moving mouth creates an impression of speech.

Even as a newborn, your baby is capable of a certain amount of cross-modal matching. She automatically will turn her eyes toward the source of a sound. If you touch her, she will look to the spot where she felt the touch. If she sees an object close at hand, she may motion toward it. But there is some question as to whether these cross-sensory connections are deliberate or reflexive in the first few months after birth.

In the 1970s psychologist T. G. R. Bower conducted

several experiments to test an infant's ability to discriminate between the senses. In one, he showed a three-week-old baby a pair of alternately flashing lights. Typically, the child quickly became bored with the lights, at which point Bower repositioned them so the infant had to look farther to the side, up or down in order to see the flash. This would recapture the baby's interest.

But if, instead of moving the lights, Bower replaced the flashes with two loud clicks originating from the same points, the babies showed no renewed interest. According to Bower, "It is almost as if the very young baby knows that something is going on in these two places in space, but doesn't really notice whether the event arrives in her mind through her ears or through her eyes."

<hr/>

D I S C O V E R Y   P L A Y

Sensory Discrimination

With your one-month-old you can play a game similar to Dr. Bower's experiments by using a jingle bell and a blinking flashlight. Concealing the bell in your hand, hold the flashlight about a foot in front of your baby. Make it blink until she grows bored with it and looks away. Then turn it off and shake your hand so the bell jingles. Does she respond to the sound, or ignore it? Try this game every few weeks to see when your baby begins to differentiate between sight and sound.

<hr/>

You have no difficulty telling the difference between a real object (such as a ball) and an illusion of that object (a reflection of the ball in a mirror), but it takes a while for your baby to develop that skill. Tufts University psychologist Emily Bushnell conducted a series of experiments in which infants were first shown a reflection of a button in a mirror and then the button itself, which they were able to touch. Bushnell found that eight-month-olds did not seem to notice a difference between the two situations. Although they reached for the buttons in both cases, they acted no more upset or interested when the button was an illusion than when it was real. The nine-and-a-half-month-olds, however, were much more intrigued by the illusory buttons than the real ones.

D I S C O V E R Y P L A Y

Illusions

Watch your baby's reactions to soap bubbles, smoke, wind and mirrors to see how she responds to illusion. If she's like most infants, she'll watch soap bubbles in fascination, but at some point she will be surprised, or even upset, that she can't really touch them. Even if she has watched herself in a mirror since she was a week old, there will come a time when she is suddenly perplexed by the reflections in the glass. This is a sign that she is developing the ability to distinguish between reality and illusion.

Oxford University researchers wanted to know if a baby who was allowed to touch an object, but not look at it, would recognize the object later just by seeing it. First they let eight-month-old babies look at two fiberglass eggs, one smooth, the other notched. The eggs were removed and then one was brought back for the baby to feel, but not see.

As the baby touched this egg, it made a bleeping sound. The egg was removed and then both were returned to the table for the baby to look at. Most infants immediately reached for the egg that bleeped and tried to make it bleep again. They recognized its *visual* shape by matching it mentally to the shape they had felt.

Psychologists at the Albert Einstein College of Medicine also have been exploring the ability of babies to relate information from one sense to another. They tested a group of one-year-olds for tactile (touch) recognition of objects. In the first phase of the test the children were allowed to look at, play with and mouth five toys for one minute. The lights were then turned out and the babies were presented with the same five objects plus five new toys with different shapes. It was so dark the babies could not see the toys, but their hands were positioned so they could feel and hold all of them.

If they were able to recognize, by feel, the toys with which they had already played, they should be more interested in exploring the unfamiliar toys. (As we'll discuss later in this chapter, babies of this age reliably prefer the unknown to the known.) As predicted, the one-year-olds spent far more time exploring the new objects than the ones they had played with earlier.

Because much of the touching was done by mouthing objects, the Einstein experiment also showed that babies can recognize shapes orally as well as manually. University of Texas psychologist Terry W. Allen found that babies as young as three months are able to differentiate between shapes they have mouthed and new shapes. Other researchers believe this ability may exist from birth.

D I S C O V E R Y   P L A Y

Tactile Recognition

Try these games with your baby to see when she can visually recognize objects she's known before only through touch (you can try this as soon as she's able to reach for objects). Equip yourself with a collection of "touchables" such as shaped teethers and rubber bath toys. Experiment with different ways to present one or two of these to your baby without her seeing them. You might hide them under a blanket or, if she'll stand for it, blindfold her.

Alternatively you can present them to her in a dark room or at night with the lights out. After she's touched and mouthed them for a minute or two, mix the toys with others that she's never played with. Let her look at the selection and see which toys she chooses. If she goes for the new toys it means she recognizes the ones she played with in the dark. This is a good example of cross-modal recognition.

Cross-modal matching also involves rhythms and spatial relationships. We all perform this skill when we watch a movie, matching the voices coming from speakers with the faces on the screen. We assume that the softer voices belong to faces seen in the distance and the louder sounds come from characters in the foreground. We match male voices with male faces, female tones with women and childish voices with children, and we notice if the soundtrack is the slightest bit out of sync with the picture.

For some time psychologists assumed that this ability developed gradually in infants, but recently they discovered that newborns perform the same audiovisual matching as adults. When babies just a few weeks old are shown indentical movies with matching and nonmatching soundtracks, they show a clear preference for the films with matching sound. University of Washington researchers Patricia Kuhl and Andrew Meltzoff have found that newborns are sensitive not just to the rhythms of speech, but also to the nuances of individual sounds. If the picture and soundtrack are mismatched even marginally, a baby will notice.

THE DEVELOPMENT OF MEMORY

It's clear from experiments like the ones just described that babies are very talented people. It's also clear that they digest and *remember* a great deal of information about the world around them. But infant memory remains one of the most controversial topics in child development circles. What do newborns remember? How long can they remember information? What kinds of information can they recall at will? Why do they remember some events better than others? These are important questions because it's impossible to learn unless you can remember. To discover what infants are capable of learning, we need to know what and how they remember.

The most basic form of memory is evident in infants just hours old and it is refined throughout life. Called habituation, it helps protect us from being overstimulated and is prompted by any sensation that persists for more than a few seconds. For example, a bright light flashed straight in your eyes will annoy you, but if the flashing light persists you get used to it. You arrive at the seashore and the sound of the waves seems deafening, but after a few minutes the noise is like background music. You enter a house in which toast has been burned and the smell seems intolerable, but within moments you no longer notice it. This is habituation.

When your newborn baby first sees a bright light or hears a loud noise, she'll startle and stare intently at the source of stimulation. Her heart will race and she may wriggle and cry. If the noise or light continues for more than a few seconds, she habituates, her heart rate returning to normal as she quiets down. If the same noise or light starts up again within the next two days, she'll ignore it, apparently remembering that it's neither threatening nor entertaining enough to get excited about. This is all part of habituation.

Your baby also can habituate to an object or image. Give her a new toy. She'll play with it for a few minutes and then lose interest. You'd say she was bored with it. Scientists would say she had habituated to the toy.

Researchers have found that most babies habituate to stimuli more easily when they're asleep or in a quiet state. They also seem to habituate more readily to tactile stimulation (being touched, stroked, hugged, etc.) than auditory stimulation (noise, changes in volume, rhythm, etc.). The older the child, the less time it takes her to habituate. Researchers at Albert Einstein College of Medicine found that three-and-one-half-month-olds can habituate to a three-dimensional geometric shape in thirty seconds; six-and-one-half-month-olds familiarize themselves with the same shape in just fifteen seconds.

D I S C O V E R Y   P L A Y

Habituation

Try an "experiment" with your own baby using two new toys. Give one toy to your child and let her play with it for about a minute. Then take it and place it next to the second toy so that both are the same distance from her and both are within her reach. She may pause momentarily to glance at the familiar toy, but she will probably devote most of her attention to the novel object.

Babies' preference for novelty has become a mainstay of studies in infant memory (as you'll see here and in the next few chapters). Researchers typically let a baby play with a toy until she grows bored with it. Then they wait a measured amount of time before showing her the toy again, next to one or two toys she's never seen. If she remembers toy number one she'll pay more attention to the new ones, so the researchers repeat this "test" at longer and longer intervals until she no longer shows a preference for the new toys. This is the signal that she's forgotten toy number one. Even very young infants who can't actually play with toys will still pay more attention to novel objects or images than ones they recognize.

This principle is something you can use in guiding your selection of toys, games and nursery objects. Your baby is likely to tire quickly of simple toys and objects that remain the same. As the following descriptions of experiments will demonstrate, those toys and objects that can be continually modified or which change slightly with use are the ones most likely to interest your infant for long periods of time.

In her studies of infant memory, Rutgers University psychologist Carolyn Rovee-Collier observes babies as young as eight weeks in their homes as they "operate" mobiles over their cribs. She uses a long ribbon to connect one of the baby's ankles to the arm from which the mobile is suspended. When the child moves that leg, the mobile jiggles in response. After a few minutes, the infant starts to kick that leg on purpose to make the mobile move.

Eventually the baby stops moving the other leg altogether and intently focuses all her attention on the leg that works the mobile. Considering that babies usually don't perform this kind of unilateral (one-sided) movement before the age of five or six months, this feat is remarkable. It shows how much infants are capable of accomplishing if their payoff is great enough.

An infant's interest in moving a mobile *she controls herself* seems almost inexhaustible. Even young babies will play this game for up to twenty minutes without losing interest. Rovee-Collier believes the mobile remains novel to the baby because it moves continually, creating entertaining patterns, shapes and visual rhythms. Most important of all, it allows the child to be an *active* participant.

Infants seem to remember the experience of moving the mobile for days afterward. When revisited and reattached to the mobile, the babies usually begin kicking almost immediately at about the same rate as they left off the day before. Not only do these babies remember the connection between the mobile and their movements, but also the precise pattern and rate of movements from the last moment they saw the mobile.

Over the years, Rutgers researchers have created many variations of this experiment to test different aspects of infant memory. They've found that:

· The day after first encountering a mobile, babies will only kick actively in response to the exact same mobile. If one of the five objects on the mobile is removed or changed, the babies will kick slightly less than predicted. If two objects are changed the babies will kick even less. The babies show no sign of recognizing the mobile if three objects are changed and will not kick at all initially. But if four or five days go by before a baby sees the mobile again, she will kick as strenuously for a new or altered mobile as she would for the original. Rovee-Collier believes this happens because the infant eventually forgets the specific individual shapes and colors of the mobile, but vaguely remembers its overall configuration.

· Infant memory, like adult memory, can be "jogged," or recalled. By two weeks after the first encounter with the mobile, most three-month-olds seem to have forgotten the experience. However, their memory can be prompted if they are shown the original mobile moving as it did when they controlled it.

If shown the mobile on the thirteenth day (without being allowed to control it), then tested the next day, babies will kick as strongly as if they'd remembered the experience all along. This "reactivation" process will work for up to a month or more with infants three months old.

· The attraction of the mobile appears to change as the infant gets older and her vision develops. Eight-week-old infants tend to look intently at a few of the objects within the mobile rather than at the mobile as a whole. By twelve weeks of age the babies are more interested in the entire mobile than in the details on each individual object.

At nine weeks, the baby prefers high-contrast black-and-white mobiles to colored ones. By four months she likes colored mobiles best and may pay special attention to particular colors. Babies of this age, for example, typically show more interest in blue than green. These details are important because, at every stage, the more a baby likes a mobile, the better she will remember it.

D I S C O V E R Y   P L A Y

Memory and Manipulation

You and your baby can both have fun with your own version of the mobile experiments. It's good exercise for the baby and gives her a toy she can manipulate even before she learns to sit or control her fingers and hands. However, to get the most out of the activity and to ensure your baby's safety, observe the following rules:

- *Never leave your baby alone while the ankle ribbon is in the crib, either attached to her or to the mobile.*
- *Select a mobile with soft hanging parts. Secure the mobile so there is no chance the baby can pull it down into the crib. Also make sure that all components of the mobile are tightly fastened so they can't fall off.*
- *Tie the ribbon loosely around your baby's ankle. You should be able to slip it off easily but the baby should not be able to push it off.*
- *Adjust the ribbon so it is taut from your baby's ankle to the mobile. The mobile should jiggle*

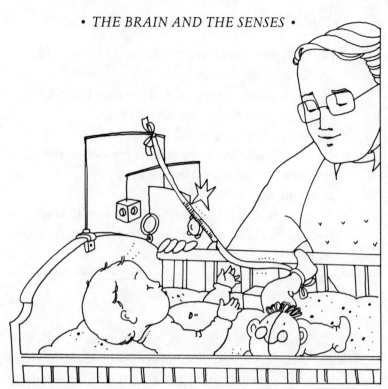

The "interactive mobile" teaches your baby about cause and effect, helps her develop body awareness and challenges her memory. Always untie the ankle ribbon and remove it from your baby's crib before you leave her alone. The mobile should be removed from the crib by five months or before your baby can sit up alone.

   slightly without dipping too forcefully when your baby kicks.
 • Switch the ribbon from one leg to the other and, occasionally, to one of her wrists so your baby can work the mobile with different limbs.
 • Alter the mobile to suit your baby's changing preferences as she gets older. The mobile should contain relatively uniform shapes with

bold, high-contrast patterns when she is eight
weeks old. By the time she is three months old
she will prefer more elaborate mobiles with
figures representing interesting objects.
• Minimize distractions when your baby is working the mobile. It may be hard for her to concentrate if there is a new face within sight or
someone is talking to her.
• Stop after fifteen minutes, or sooner if your
baby gets fussy. Remember, this is play, not
work.

Watch carefully as your baby performs this and other
activities. With each new accomplishment she will share
her delight with you. That's your cue to add more variety
and challenge to her play and provide her with more
games in which she can be an active participant. Remember that all of your baby's activities can bring out new
discoveries. For a baby, discovery *is* play.

· VI ·

Hearing

Your baby's hearing is fully mature at birth. A newborn can distinguish even subtle differences between sounds that are familiar and sounds she has not heard before.

Researchers in Boston tested this ability in a group of babies less than four days old. While lying at rest, each infant listened to two tapes of rattle sounds. One sound was produced by soybeans in a plastic container. The other sound, similar but slightly higher in pitch, was produced by a container with fava beans. The infants quickly got used to the first rattle they heard and turned away. As soon as the sound made by the other beans was played, their interest rekindled and they turned toward it. You can try this discovery game with your own baby using two similar rattles or noisemakers.

Not only can newborns normally hear as well as adults, they also can track the direction and source of sounds. If you gently snap your fingers near a baby's right ear, she hears the sound first in her right ear, then a fraction of a second later in her left. This time lag tells her that the sound is on her right, and she will move her head toward it.

She'll also turn her eyes toward the sound, which tells you that she expects to be able to *see* source of the sound, too. Considering that newborn babies have never actually seen anything produce a noise, it's amazing that they make this connection. This is cross-modal matching in action.

Since the earliest and most consistent sounds babies normally hear are their parents' voices, this audiovisual connection probably plays an important part in the bonding between infants and their key caretakers. It also helps babies learn what communication is all about.

Babies don't have to see to learn to talk. However, the sight of people around them applying their communication skills probably helps provide babies with a broader notion of what speech is all about. As they simultaneously watch and hear words being fashioned around them, they begin to understand that speaking is what people do to send messages to each other.

The fact that infants naturally prefer the human voice to other types of sounds probably helps them learn to talk. Studies show that two-week-old infants smile more often and more regularly when they hear someone talking than they do in response to other forms of stimulation. When an older infant, busy learning a new task, looks for approval to her mother, the pleased sound of Mom's voice is generally sufficient reward to keep the baby working at her chore, even if Mom is out of sight.

Not all human voices are equal in the infant's view. A baby less than a month old would rather listen to her mother's normal speaking voice than anyone else's. But if the mother's voice is unnaturally distorted, the infant may cry in protest. Numerous studies have shown that infants also can discriminate between two strangers' voices and between male and female voices. Given a choice between listening to a man or woman, they will choose the female voice almost every time. Some experts suggest this is because the baby gets to know her mother's voice during pregnancy and then identifies all female voices with the mother.

Although no one really understands why babies like high-pitched voices, men, women and children seem to know intuitively that they do. Just listen to the next person who talks to your baby. He or she will almost certainly, and perhaps quite unconsciously, talk in a high-pitched, somewhat breathless voice—a more feminine voice.

Watch how your baby reacts. She probably will come alive, smiling and wriggling as if she knows that this special way of talking, unlike the speech used between other people, is meant exclusively for her. Even if you're in the next room and call to your baby in this voice, she'll have the same reaction. It is her own private language, and when you use it you make her feel prized and special.

Through everyday family conversation, babies quickly build an enormous repertoire of sounds which they can identify and differentiate. By the age of one month newborns can tell the difference between most of the subtle sounds of speech, including individual vowels and consonants.

In time babies start linking certain facial expressions with specific sounds, words and phrases, a process that helps them discover the emotional potential of speech. In 1983 researchers at Rutgers University set out to determine how old infants are when they learn the difference between happy voices and sad voices.

From previous studies, they knew that six- or seven-month-olds react differently to positive and negative tones of voice and older infants have a negative reaction to sad and angry faces and voices. In this study, they worked with babies aged three and five months. First, the infants were shown slides of a woman posing with either a happy or sad facial expression. Simultaneously, they listened to an audiocassette of a woman speaking in the matching emotion. When the babies grew bored the tape changed to the opposite vocal emotion, so the children were listening to sad talk while looking at a happy face or vice versa.

Only the five-month-olds clearly seemed to understand what had happened, coming to attention and studying the slide. The younger babies startled briefly at the change in voice, but did not show any renewed interest.

FROM LISTENING TO SPEAKING

You may be surprised to learn that infants actually can "talk" more in their early months than when they grow up. That is to say, they can produce more varied sounds. The vocal capability of newborns contains the essential sounds of every language on earth, including many exotic clicking, nasal and guttural tones used by remote Oriental cultures and African tribes. Moreover, newborns seem to have an innate understanding of the structures of these languages.

By minutely analyzing videotapes of infants, researchers have found that babies just twelve hours old will move precisely in time to the words and syllables of languages as different as English and Chinese, although they do not move in time to regular tapping or isolated vowel sounds.

Babies are even able to differentiate verbal units in a foreign language that their parents hear as single sounds. Clearly, children the world over are born with the basic equipment they need to talk to each other. It's only later that we lose our vocal equality.

Jerome Kagan, a Harvard authority on child development, claims that the newborn's vast linguistic ability is but one example of how complex—and complete—the central nervous system of the human is at birth. He argues that the brain in fact does not grow by expansion, but rather by a kind of "pruning" of unnecessary nerve synapses, which allows the most necessary structures to become stronger.

Through this process, the baby's vocal repertoire narrows after the first half year. She begins eliminating the sounds she doesn't need. There is no reinforcement for using sounds that she doesn't hear other people using, and she becomes so preoccupied with the challenge of two-way conversation that the extra vocalizations drop by the wayside.

Soon after a baby stops making specific sounds, she loses the ability to produce them. This is why Americans grow up unable to pronounce the African clicks they made as infants and why Japanese adults have so much difficulty with consonants such as "l" or "r," which they babbled quite easily as babies. This may also explain why children born to parents of different nationalities naturally become multilingual, while the parents themselves may never become fluent in each other's languages.

The quantity as well as the quality of your baby's babbling is influenced by her surroundings. Social and emotional rewards bring out her talkativeness. Developmental psychologists have found that infants will talk back to tape recordings of their mother's voices.

If you smile, cuddle, stroke or converse with your child whenever she speaks, she's bound to keep on talking. (Note that the reinforcement does not need to be verbal. Children of nonspeaking parents generally babble just as much as children of parents who do speak.)

There's an important difference, however, between talking to a baby and talking at her. Only conversation that involves her as a participant will encourage her to talk. This means if you are having a discussion with your older child while holding your baby, the baby will stop babbling.

Babies will stop making sounds when they hear tape recordings of their own voices. They join in only when they hear themselves being invited by the pattern of the discussion. Generally, children who talk the most have parents who not only include them, but also respond enthusiastically to "conversations" that the children themselves initiate. These parents bring out their babies' verbal skills from an early age.

D I S C O V E R Y P L A Y

Hearing and Listening

These games will show you how important sound stimuli are to your baby and how sensitively she reacts to them. They will not tell you if your baby's hearing is normal. If you have any concern that your baby has a hearing problem, talk to your doctor about it. If any

question remains, the baby should be tested by a
professional who specializes in this area. No child is
too young to be tested.

- Let your baby show you how well she listens
  to sounds. Repeat a single syllable (for example, *"un"* or *"go"*) over and over for several
  seconds, until she appears to lose interest.
  Then switch to a different sound (perhaps
  "boo" or *"la"*), and see if she becomes attentive again. That reaction tells you she understands the difference between the sounds.

- Change the pitch of your voice while speaking
  to your baby. See if she reacts differently when
  you talk to her in a very high pitch from when
  you use a very low-pitched voice. Which does
  she seem to prefer?

- Stand in front of your baby and move your lips
  without making sounds while someone of the
  opposite sex talks out loud. The other person
  should be hidden out of your baby's sight.
  Does your baby seem to detect the incongru-
  ence?

- Talk to your baby directly, then talk to someone else in the room or pretend you are talking
  to someone on the phone. What does your
  baby do when you switch the focus of your
  conversation from her to someone else?

- Gather together some audiocassettes or records with different kinds of music on them
  (classical, ballads, folk, polkas, rock). Play
  short segments of each type of music (60-90

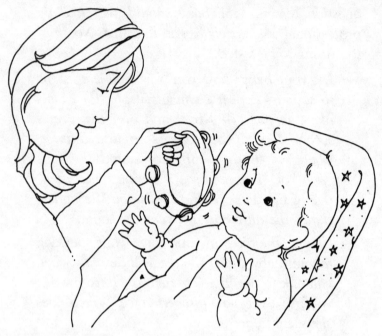

Introduce your baby to rhythm and musical tones by playing simple instruments for her.

seconds) and observe your baby's reactions carefully.

Can you detect her favorite kind of music? Are there some types she dislikes? Repeat this game at regular intervals to see if her reactions change. Use the information you gain this way to select new tapes and records for your child's personal audio library.

· VII ·

Seeing

To a casual observer, it will seem as though a newborn infant can barely see. The truth is, although your baby has distinct limitations at first, she also has some remarkable visual abilities. Being aware of both will help you enrich her experience visually. You'll also enjoy watching her visual development yourself.

Even before birth your baby has distinct visual abilities. If a bright light is flashed alongside the mother's abdomen during the final months of pregnancy, the fetus often will startle in response. If the bright flashing light persists for more than a few moments, the fetus stops moving entirely. If the bright light is replaced by a soft one, the fetus will move gently toward it, gradually becoming more active the longer the light remains.

Your baby's sensitivity to light intensifies after birth. She will squint if the light in the room shifts suddenly and shut her eyes tightly in protest against an extremely bright light. Initially she reacts only to relatively gradual changes in lightness and brightness. Most newborns cannot react to flashes that occur more frequently than one per second. However, during the first few weeks, the baby's reaction time quickly speeds up.

As a newborn, your baby has much more to look at than she ever encountered in the womb, but she has certain visual limitations that protect her from being over-whelmed. The most important of these is her restricted field of vision. At birth she can only focus on objects within a range of about eight to ten inches from her eyes. The far reaches remain a blur to her until about four months.

When she is alert and concentrating, however, your baby can see very clearly within her range of focus. She is able to distinguish the details of your face and objects or patterns that you show her. She may study them so intently that she will even stop sucking to watch an interesting distraction during feeding.

The first weeks and months are critical to an infant's developing vision, which is why pediatricians try to detect any eye problems as soon as possible after birth. Children who are born with cataracts or other severe visual limita-tions will never be able to establish normal vision unless the problem is corrected within the first six months. After this point, the brain seems to lose the capacity to process visual information normally.

VISUAL TRACKING

Babies with normal vision can track moving objects as soon as they are born, but this ability is limited at first and develops gradually with practice. It will probably take your baby a month or two of practice before she can keep her eye smoothly and constantly on a moving object. Move a large picture or a sheet of paper marked with a high-contrast design (such as black against white or dark blue against yellow) across your baby's field of vision and she will have a much easier time following it than if you dangle a small toy in front of her.

Look carefully and you'll notice that her eye movements are relatively smooth when she is following the large, flat design. Her eyes will move in a jerky motion, as if trying to catch up, when she attempts to track the smaller, three-dimensional toy.

D I S C O V E R Y   P L A Y

Visual Tracking

You can gauge your baby's tracking ability as it develops. Several toys specifically designed for this purpose are on the market, including see-through rods or boxes with distinct forms inside. As you tilt the toy, the movement of the form inside catches your baby's attention; the game is to see how long she can track it.

You can set up the same game on your own, using a black-and-white pattern or object as the target that you move back and forth and up and down. At first your baby will only be able to track very slow move-

*ments within short distances. As she gets older you
can increase the speed and range and try a variety of
different directions. Soon she will be able to track a
ball rolling all the way across the room. Always remember, however, that this is a play activity, not a test.*

Notice how your newborn seems to move her head as
she tries to follow a moving object with her eyes. You're
not imagining this. Despite her minimal coordination, your
baby knows that her eyes and body are connected, and she
tries her best to put this connection into action. Her head
jerks awkwardly to the sides and even up and down as she
tries to keep the object in sight. There is evidence that,
although a newborn's limited muscular coordination prevents her from tracking objects effectively, she can tell
where objects are located around her.

More to the point, studies show that babies just a week
or two old can tell if they are in the line of fire of something coming toward them. Some tests were done with
illusory shadows projected from screens so the babies
thought that flying objects were approaching them. Others
used an image of a rotating board projected in such a way
that the infants thought it would hit them on their noses
as it spun around. In no case were the children in any real
danger, but the effect was very real. In every one of these
experiments, the babies pulled away from the moving images in order to protect themselves.

D I S C O V E R Y   P L A Y

Avoidance

You can probably observe this talent in your own baby by putting her in your lap or an infant seat and bringing an object—or your hand—directly toward her face. She will try to defend herself against it by squinting, pulling her head away or trying to put her hands up. If, instead, you move the object on a path that would take it just past her face, making it a near miss, she will calmly watch it pass without flinching.

The fascinating—and still unanswered—question is, how do babies acquire this protective defense? Few newborn babies have had the experience of being hit by a flying object or smacked on the nose by a revolving board, but their reactions in these tests suggest they innately understand the threat of a collision. The tests also indicate that babies have a built-in gauge of the distance between themselves and the world around them. Newborns are not nearly as defenseless as they appear!

COLOR

Another aspect of vision that develops gradually in babies is the ability to differentiate color. Until fairly recently, the scientific community assumed that children were unable to identify colors until they learned to talk. Researchers believed that children had to be taught one color from another through the process of "labeling," and that this couldn't happen until the children knew language (many early-education primers still refer to "learning your colors").

But recent research has proven that babies are born with a primitive ability to discern hue and, before six months have passed, can identify every color of the rainbow.

Most evidence indicates that newborn babies are very sensitive to contrast, such as black versus white, and to the brightness of color. This means that your baby can tell the difference between a crisp yellow daffodil and a deep crimson cherry in the pattern of her nursery curtains (if the patterns are close enough to her eyes). She may also be able to read the hue in some primary colors. But the newborn's eye is not developed enough to respond to the subtleties of most hues until the fourth or fifth month.

Canadian psychologists Russell Adams and Daphne Maurier tested newborns and two-month-olds to find out how sensitive they were to contrast between dark and light. The babies were shown a series of checkerboards in which the contrast between the light and dark squares ranged from 3 percent to 27 percent.

The newborns, tested within the first week after birth, were only able to detect a pattern in checkerboards with more than 5 percent contrast. Two-month-olds, on the other hand, had no trouble identifying the pattern until the contrast dropped to 3 percent. Apparently, sensitivity to light and dark increases as the baby gets older. By the time we reach adulthood, we are able to detect contrasts smaller than .3 percent.

In 1975 Mark Bornstein conducted a color preference test using light projections in eight different hues. The amount of time each child looked at each color was timed. Regardless of the order in which colors were presented, the children all seemed to prefer the same colors: red and shades of blue were favored most, followed by purple, orange, yellow and green.

The infants' color preferences generally matched the colors preferred by a sample of adults. The only significant difference was that the babies liked yellow more than green, while the adults preferred green.

D I S C O V E R Y   P L A Y

Color Preferences

What about your baby? What colors does she prefer? You may be able to find out when she is about three months old by presenting her with identical objects of different colors (a red block and a green block, for example). See if she looks at one longer than the other or tries to reach for one in particular.

You can vary the color combinations as long as the choices are identical in every way except color. (If one is larger than the other or has a different pattern, your baby may base her choice on size or design rather than hue.) You may want to minimize the differences and extend your color options by using pieces of colored paper. Large sheets of origami paper or construction paper work well and are about the right size to hold an infant's attention. You can repeat this activity periodically to find out whether your baby's preferences are permanent or change as she gets older.

In later experiments, Bornstein established that four-month-old babies can sort hues across the spectrum into blues, greens, yellows and reds. First he held up a vivid primary color, such as bright blue, until the child grew bored with it. He then showed the baby variations of blue that moved closer and closer to green on the spectrum.

As long as the color stayed within the range that adults would call blue, the baby remained bored with the game, but as soon as the hues moved into the green family, her interest was rekindled. Babies in this experiment showed the same shifts of interest with each major shift between color families.

Even though the spectrum of hues, like the rainbow, is continuous, it seems that babies divide colors into specific groups just as adults do.

D I S C O V E R Y   P L A Y

Color Differentiation

It might be fun for you to try these color games with your own infant, using sets of colored-paper swatches that are available at most art supply stores. (These are fairly large sturdy sheets of paper that are richer in color than the small paint samples you find at hardware stores.) Select pairs of different colors that are about the same brightness and intensity, and show them to your baby when she is alert and in a quiet mood. Pull a selection of colors that range from one primary hue to the next, from red to purple, for example. Show the first color to your baby until she loses interest, then show the others one by one. See if you can tell which color revives her interest. You can keep playing the game as your child gets older to see if her reactions change with age.

Eventually, as she starts to talk, you can use this activity to help her discover the verbal names of the colors she already knows so well.

EARLY PATTERN PREFERENCES

Notice how your baby likes to look at certain patterns more than others: the picture on her wall, the stripes in her bedding or the designs in her nursery curtains. Maybe it's the face on the shampoo label that captures her gaze at bathtime.

As you watch your infant at play, you probably will discover the patterns that are most attractive to her. If you watch for this as she gets older, you'll see that her preferences for patterns change. Remarkably, all babies go through the same general changes.

Canadian psychologists tested pattern preferences in babies at three weeks, eight weeks and fourteen weeks.

At birth your baby favors simple linear patterns, but by around three months she becomes fascinated with facial features and circular patterns.

While lying in a special chamber, each baby was shown two cards at a time while an observer recorded her eye movements to find out which cards she preferred. The cards each contained checkerboard patterns ranging in complexity from four squares to 576 squares.

The psychologists found that the three-week-old babies preferred the checkerboards with the fewest squares—the least complex ones.

The eight-week-old group preferred the moderately complex cards, and the oldest group clearly preferred the most complex checkerboards. Newborns, who are least developed, apparently like simpler patterns, while older babies search out more complicated images.

Other researchers have tested this generalization with many other types of patterns, and it seems to hold true. With rare exceptions, all babies from birth to six months prefer some sort of pattern to a plain surface. However, newborns also love brightness and big shapes, so if you show your one-week-old a huge cutout of a scarlet bear, she may well concentrate more on that than on a pale blue-and-white checkerboard you hold up next to it.

There is also some evidence that certain types of patterns, regardless of their complexity, are especially appealing to infants at certain ages. Case Western Reserve researcher Robert Fantz found that newborns tend to look longest at stripes and other straight-line patterns, but after two months they like circular patterns better.

By three months, he found, babies will look at a bull's-eye eight times longer than at stripes. Likewise, newborns prefer to look at patterns of squares that are arranged along a grid, but by four months they would much rather look at squares arranged in circular patterns.

You can take advantage of these findings when selecting the decorations for your baby's nursery. Large black-and-white paintings or posters with vertical and horizontal straight-line patterns will appeal most to your newborn.

Replace them with colored circular designs toward the end of her second month. You can even make the designs yourself, using paint, crayons or cutout pieces of paper. This way you can change them easily when your infant loses interest in them.

Remember to place the pictures where your child can see them. A crib bumper with see-through pockets provides a perfect display case. You can also hang the pictures

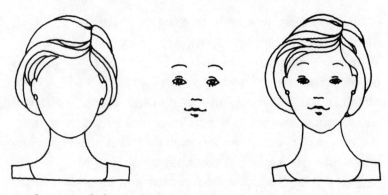

At first your baby is most attracted to the edges of your face. By three months she is most interested in your facial features, and by five months she sees how all of your features fit together as a whole.

above the changing table or, later, in your kitchen within view of the high chair.

Another favorite image for babies is the human face. At almost all ages children love to look at faces, but the specific attraction changes as they get older. In general, your baby will be drawn toward more details and increasing complexity as she gets older.

As a newborn she likes simple dots and angles, and gazes most at the edges of your face. At about seven weeks she becomes enthralled with the crisp geometric bull's-eye pattern of your eyes. Around three months she's involved with all your facial features, though not so much the shape of your face or hair. When you are talking or moving your eyes, you become much more attractive to her. As she approaches her fifth month, your baby is happiest when she can see your whole head, and by eight months she begins to notice individual expressions and subtle differences between one face and another.

Some experts believe that the way an infant looks at a pattern determines which designs she likes best. At birth your baby will scan randomly, looking here and there at a picture or a blank sheet without focusing closely on details.

By one month she'll find one particular point in the picture to study. She won't be happy unless the picture offers some complexity, and she'll fuss and cry if confronted by a blank sheet. By two months she loses her fascination with single details and works an image more methodically, looking first at one point, then another. She now is more involved with the internal features of a picture than the edges.

D I S C O V E R Y   P L A Y

Patterns and Shapes

Let your own baby show you how she looks at things. Take two large pieces of white paper. Using wide, dark marker pens, draw a large square on one; on the other draw a large square with two small squares inside it.

Which drawing does your baby look at longer? If she's just a month old, she will probably prefer the empty box. If she's two months or older, the other drawing is likely to hold her attention longer.

Infants seem to grasp many of the abstract qualities of images. Even before they learn to talk, they can demonstrate this. In one study, infants first listened to tones that were either pulsing or continuous, then were shown two lines—one broken and the other continuous.

The babies who had heard the pulsing noise stared at the broken line. The children who had heard the continuous sound stared at the solid line. They seemed to understand the meaning of the concepts—continuous and broken—even if they could not describe them.

D I S C O V E R Y   P L A Y

Continuity

You can play similar discovery games with your baby by mixing and matching a variety of musical and visual stimuli for her. For example, play a rousing march or passage from a symphony. Then show your child a selection of pictures or designs which, to your mind, complement or contradict the feeling of the music. See which of the pictures attract your infant's attention.

Does she choose the images which you think match the mood of the music, or does she have her own ideas on the subject? Remember, there are no right or wrong answers. The object is to bring you and your child closer together by helping you experience the world through each other's eyes.

Play this game only when your baby is alert, quiet

and interested. Try it with a range of musical and visual cues that reflect happiness, sadness and anger, as well as dynamic qualities such as smoothness, bounciness and staccato.

SPACE AND FORM

How does your tiny baby know that the ball six inches away from her is the same size when it is three yards away? It looks much bigger when it's closer, but babies are rarely confused when real objects are used (as opposed to drawings or photographs).

Psychologist T. G. R. Bower tested infants between the ages of six weeks and eight weeks to see how they reacted to these spatial illusions. Bower first showed the babies a twelve-inch cube placed behind a screen about a yard away. If the babies turned their heads when the screen was raised to reveal the cube, a woman would pop up and, to the babies' delight, play peekaboo. Very quickly the babies learned that they had to turn their heads and look at that particular cube in order to play peekaboo.

Once they clearly understood the game, Bower started changing cubes. One time the screen would rise to reveal a cube three times the size of the original, but three times farther away. Another time the screen would open on the bigger cube placed at the same distance as the original. And a third time the screen would show the original cube placed three times farther away than it had been during the training sessions. If photographs were taken of the various possibilities, the larger cube, placed far away, would look the same as the original.

But the babies were not taken in by this illusion. They

responded far more promptly and reliably to the original cube, even though it was farther away, than they did to the larger cube. Somehow the babies knew the difference between real size and apparent size.

Considering the limited experiences of tiny infants, the certainty with which they view their world is remarkable. You'd think it would take some time for them to understand that objects stay the same size when they change position. Apparently, babies are born with the visual and mental equipment they need to make this and other spatial equations.

Infants are just as perceptive about the dimensionality of objects. Imagine a series of photographs of a cube, each photograph showing the cube in a different position. In one picture all you see is a square because the cube is viewed head on. In all the others, the cube has six edges

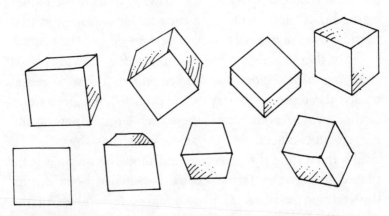

Objectively speaking, this cube looks like a different object each time it changes position, but even very young babies understand that it's the same cube seen from different perspectives.

D I S C O V E R Y   P L A Y

Distance Perception

Play a similar discovery game with your own baby when she's about five months old. Place a small toy within her reach on a table at her eye level. She probably will try to grab it. But if you place a much larger toy beyond her reach, she won't grasp for it. She may reach, as if to point, but you can't fool her into thinking it's near enough for her to touch.

of various lengths with shadows of differing shapes and intensities. When you look at these photographs you know that they all depict the same cube, but how do you know?

Objectively speaking, no two of these images are alike. Do you simply recognize them all because you have examined cubes in different positions? Or do you have some innate understanding of the way objects appear in space? Your baby will show you how *she* perceives this if you show her pictures of the cube in all its various positions. That's what the scientists have done.

In one experiment babies aged eight weeks to twenty weeks were shown the cube in one position for thirty seconds; then the lights were turned out. When they came on again, the cube was in a different position. The babies viewed the cube in eight different positions, with lights out between each showing.

If these children thought the cube changed as it moved, they should have remained interested in each successive image. But they quickly lost interest in the whole game, just as they would if the same exact image were flashed eight different times. Regardless of the changing positions, these babies figured out that they were watching the same cube over and over again. Very boring!

Given your infant's built-in sensitivity to the three-dimensional world, it's small wonder that she likes real objects better than flat images such as paintings or drawings. This preference develops gradually over the first two months as her eyesight improves and she begins exploring her surroundings more actively.

DISCOVERY PLAY

Dimensionality

Let your baby show you what she likes to look at as you play together. Offer her a choice between flat (two-dimensional) and three-dimensional objects of about equal proportions. For example, show her a picture of an apple and a real apple, a photograph of a head and a doll's head, a drawing of a triangle and a triangular block, a flat picture and a picture book. Watch her reactions to see what effect an extra dimension adds.

Learning how your child perceives the world around her is an essential part of Discovery Play. Equip your home with a wide array of pictures, books, designs and objects from which she can pick and choose. Pay attention to the direction of her gaze. Watch for the images that make her smile.

Remember, there are no right or wrong choices. At this stage of the game, the whole world is a work of art to your baby.

· VIII ·

Touching

Your brand-new baby has a remarkable sensitivity to touch. The way you pick her up and move her about can have a dramatic effect on her mood and her interactions with you. She can sense when you touch her lovingly and when you are annoyed or disinterested. She can feel the difference between rough and gentle handling. She knows when you're being playful and when you're all business, when you're angry and when you're sad. She'll quickly let you know how she likes to be touched and handled best.

Being touched may be more than just a pleasurable sensation for newborns. Research indicates it might be essential for their growth and development. Studies of other cultures show that babies who receive plenty of physical stimulation grow at a steady rate for the first months, even when food, clothing and health care are lacking.

In one study in the United States, premature babies who received extra stroking and whose limbs were gently moved gained 47 percent more weight than premature babies who were handled in the usual fashion. The babies who were handled more also appeared more alert while awake, progressed more rapidly in their behavioral development and seemed to have more regular sleeping-waking cycles.

There are no studies, however, that demonstrate a difference several years later between children who received extra physical and sensory stimulation during infancy and those who did not, and there is no proof that this kind of stimulation will make a difference in babies who are born after a full-term pregnancy.

By some fortuitous arrangement with nature, it seems that babies are immune to pain during the actual birth process. This "design" permits a baby to endure the pressures and manipulations required for her to move through the birth canal.

When she reaches the outside world and shrieks her greeting, she cries not in pain but in a kind of shock. It takes her several hours to sort out the comforting sensations of touch from the painful ones. By the end of her first day, however, your baby's sense of touch is equal to yours, and a threshold of pain is established that will remain with her for the rest of her life.

This delay of sensitivity does not extend to your baby's response to heat and cold. Newborns are not able to control their internal temperature very well, and they feel changes in outside temperature much more keenly than adults.

Your child will let you know promptly when she is too hot or too cold. In fact, according to one researcher, this is the fourth most common reason why babies cry. (The other reasons, in order, are hunger, pain and a nervous startle reaction that seems to occur spontaneously.)

Whether your baby was born full-term or prematurely, she needs a lot of touching during the first months of life.

Everyday activities such as diaper changing, clothing, bathing, kissing, lifting and stroking all provide opportunities for tactile stimulation. Take advantage of these moments to establish as much rapport with your infant as possible through touching.

D I S C O V E R Y   P L A Y

Touch

There are many different ways you can play with your baby through touch. Try these discovery games during quiet moments:

- *Touch your baby in varying rhythms. Play music at the same time, gently stroking or patting her in time with the beat. Vary the patterns of your strokes to make circles, squares, dots, dashes and long sinuous lines as you move along the skin over her abdomen and back.*

- *Rock or lift your baby as you stroke her to provide both tactile and vestibular (balance) stimulation at the same time.*

- *Use touch to encourage her to discover all the movements her body can make. Gently lift, rotate and bend her arms, legs, hands and feet. Help her extend her fingers and toes into a reach.*

- *Introduce textures to her. Stroke her on one side with terrycloth and on the other side with satin. Let her explore the textures on her own as well.*

- *Use touch games to help your baby discover shapes. Roll a small ball up and down her abdomen or lightly stroke her with a block so she can feel the edges.*

The most sensitive areas of your baby's body are her mouth, eyes, face, palms, soles and genital area, so be especially gentle there. Also, consider her frame of mind before you try these touching games. If she is sleepy, keep the activity smooth and soothing. If she's wide awake and eager for action, step up your pace to match her mood.

*Make sure you know her threshold of activity
and stimulation and don't violate it. It's very easy
to push a game when you're having fun, but be
careful not to push your baby beyond her limits.
Some infants simply can't take a lot of excitement. If your baby has this kind of temperament,
let her set the pace. When she loses interest,
respect her wishes and slow down.*

Many parents become anxious as their babies start to
move out and explore the world on their own. Hands
reach into everything, objects go into the mouth, and there
is a constant temptation for parents to restrain their babies. But these forays into taste, texture, shape and size are
just as important to your baby as the loving touches she
receives from you. Of course you need to monitor what
goes into her mouth to be sure she doesn't swallow anything harmful, but don't be overzealous in maintaining
order. Your child can learn a lot about the world by mouthing and handling small portions of it.

CALMING THROUGH TOUCH

Touch can also be an invaluable tool for calming your
baby when she is irritable or upset. Dr. T. Berry Brazelton
suggests a sequence of consolation techniques for comforting newborns who are crying for no apparent reason. Try
this sequence with your baby when she cries and see which
she reacts to most favorably. Be aware that the best way to
quiet some hypersensitive babies is to avoid stimulation of
all kinds, including touching, so lay her down on her back

first for a few moments to see if she quiets herself. If that doesn't work, try the following sequence:

1. Talk to her in a gentle tone. Try singing a lullaby or reading a poem. The regular rhythm of your voice can have a very soothing effect.
2. Next, simply place a hand on her abdomen or head. Sometimes all she needs is the tactile reassurance that you are there.
3. If she is still miserable, pick her up and hold her lightly or rock her in your arms.
4. Next comes cuddling. Hold your baby close to your chest. Most babies respond to this position by nuzzling gently—and irresistibly—into the crook of your neck.
5. If human contact doesn't work, a pacifier or bottle may be the answer. Even though your baby isn't hungry, the process of sucking can be very comforting.
6. The last resort is swaddling. Wrap her tightly in a blanket so her arms and legs are secure. This provides maximum tactile stimulation and, for some babies, is soothing.

· IX ·

Taste and Smell

As any parent quickly discovers, the urge to eat is a primary force in every newborn's life. Until recently, most people assumed that this drive was fueled purely by hunger without much regard for flavor. But this belief changed with the discovery that taste buds are one of the first sense organs to develop in fetuses. Based on studies in animals, researchers think that fetuses are able to taste and smell the amniotic fluid surrounding them during the last three months of pregnancy.

By the time she is born, your baby is even more sensitive to odors than you are. She also shows very definite preferences for certain smells. Wave a cotton swab dabbed with vanilla or banana flavoring under her nose, and she may smack her lips and suck in delight. If you tried the same trick with the smell of rotten eggs, sour milk or vinegar, she'd probably turn her head, hold her breath, sneeze, squirm, cry or spit up in disgust. (We don't recommend this experiment!)

Researchers have conducted hundreds of tests of this kind with infants less than one day old who had never tasted or smelled food of any kind. They found that newborns universally love the smells of fruit, butter, vanilla and other scents that adults generally find pleasing. Tiny babies universally seem to dislike the same rotten, fishy, acidic and acrid smells that most adults hate.

Of all the odors available, the smell of breast milk is the most compelling to a newborn baby. Within two weeks after birth, a sleeping baby will turn instinctively toward the breast pad of any mother. She is drawn to the scent of milk regardless of its source. But by six weeks the same infant is able to discriminate between odors so well she will respond only to the scent of her own mother's breast pad.

That singular smell is the only one relevant to her, so she ignores the scent of all other mothers. By the way, the "scent connection" works both ways. Within forty-eight hours after birth, over half of all mothers can identify, by smell alone, their baby's bassinet from others. Many mothers can do this within the first six hours.

D I S C O V E R Y   P L A Y

Smell

Let your baby show you which smells she likes best.
Researchers in this area say that scented stickers,
"scratch'n'sniff" patches, aromatic candles and many

other scented products are perfectly safe for you to expose to your newborn. See if you like the same scents she does!

Try to incorporate the discovery of smells into your daily activities as well. When cooking, for example, let your child sniff the ingredients before they are mixed. When you go outside for a walk, crush pine needles or flower petals for her to sample. Obviously, you'll want to stay away from harsh, toxic chemicals such as gasoline, turpentine, bleach and so forth. Search for the smells that please you. These will also be the safest and most pleasurable for your baby.

Some scientists believe the baby's acute sense of smell is what really lies behind the "security blanket." According to this theory, a baby can recognize her own scent in any blanket, toy or piece of clothing she keeps close to herself.

By bringing this scent with her as she moves about, she carries along the comfortable sense of being home and at peace. The scent on the object, in other words, is what supplies her security.

Eventually your baby will latch onto a particular toy, blanket or piece of clothing as her own security object. You can help her discover the magic in this by giving her something soft and easy to carry that will pick up her scent. Our favorite is a fabric square that you can easily make yourself.

Start with a one-foot square of soft flannel. Sew a wide satin ribbon over the edges. Give this to your baby early

A favorite blanket or toy can help your baby develop a sense of security and comfort when you're not around.

in infancy. Let her sleep with it. Bring it with her in the carriage or stroller on walks. Let her play with it (she'll love crumpling it up and rubbing her face on the soft fabric) and don't wash it any more than you absolutely have to. This way it will retain your baby's scent. Once she gets used to her security blanket it will help her fall asleep on her own and comfort her when she's upset.

Newborns are highly selective when it comes to flavor as well as scent. By putting drops of substances such as sugar, quinine, salt and citric acid on the tongues of newborns, researchers discovered that infants love sweetness and dislike bitter, sour and salty tastes. They have a remarkable ability to discriminate among the different varieties of sweetness. Your baby, for example, can tell which is lactose (the sugar in milk), fructose (the sugar in fruit) and glucose (the sugar used in cooking). How well can you distinguish among these three types of sweetness?

Scientists at Brown University wanted to learn if there was a particular concentration of sweetness that babies liked best. They worked with babies one to three days old, several hours after their last feeding (this delay ensured that the infants were hungry). Each baby was fed four solutions with different concentrations of sugar. A special nipple was used which measured the intensity of the babies' sucking. The sweeter the solution, the harder the babies sucked. These tiny infants could discern the relative sweetness of their food as accurately as any adult.

As your baby grows up she gradually acquires the taste for a broad variety of flavors. Sweetness, however, will reign as her favorite throughout childhood. This can cause dietary problems unless you are careful. Once she starts eating solid foods, she may lose her interest in exploring new tastes if the foods she gets contain too much sugar. This can limit the variety of her diet and may prevent her from getting all the nutrients she needs.

So try to encourage as much experimentation as possible (although you need to exercise some restraint when first introducing her to a foreign food that might cause an allergic reaction). As she first learns to feed herself, let her touch the food with her fingers to experience its texture. Don't be too quick to clean her up unless she is more interested in playing than eating.

These pleasure senses—taste and smell—help your baby establish an interesting and stimulating relationship with the world and people around her. So give her as many opportunities as you can, within safe limits, to exercise these senses each and every day.

Let her discover the sensuous as well as the functional side of life. What better time than infancy to learn to appreciate pleasure!

· X ·

Coordination

and

Control

How do you measure your baby's development? If you're like most parents, you focus on motor skills. You wait with baited breath for the moment when she first rolls over. Carefully, you record the dates when she first sits, crawls, stands and walks. You anxiously review the developmental charts to measure your baby's progress against the averages. You worry if she's not crawling by the date on the charts and, if she takes a step ahead of schedule, you feel a surge of pride.

Why do parents universally show such concern over the motor development of babies, when most experts believe there is no connection between your baby's rate of motor development and her intellectual development? Probably because this is the easiest area of development to observe.

You cannot know precisely when your baby begins to understand words or differentiate among colors, but it's easy to pinpoint the minute when she first sits up, and it is understandable for you to be impressed by changes you can see for yourself.

There is an even better reason for excitement over your baby's motor development: it has an enormous impact on the way she experiences life. Each new skill makes her a more active participant in her world and signals another step toward maturity. As important as her mental and sensory development are, it's the ability to stand and walk that carries her from infancy to toddlerhood.

Babies often seem to develop new abilities overnight. One day your infant can barely lift her head, the next day she is miraculously rolling over. For months she can only crawl, then suddenly she decides to get up and walk.

The truth is, motor development occurs much more gradually than this. When we focus so much attention on the appearance of key abilities like sitting and walking, we often miss the many smaller advances that babies make every day. No matter how small, each new motor achievement your baby makes is important.

There is a vital order to the way she acquires these incremental motor skills. Not until she has mastered the necessary preliminary abilities can she execute the big moves, which is why she may get frustrated if you try to teach her a new game or activity too soon. Also, when an infant is pushed or trained to perform at a level for which she's not ready, she may miss some essential intermediate developmental steps.

It's important to understand that babies tend to concentrate very heavily on developing one motor skill at a time.

Because of this it may appear that your infant has stopped developing, or even regressed, in one area while she is struggling with another. For example, once she takes her first step, she may "forget" how to crawl.

You may also find that your baby masters motor skills in an order different from other babies, sometimes skipping whole steps. For example, she may figure out how to walk without crawling first.

As long as she is designing her *own* learning patterns, there is no reason for you to worry about her departure from the "normal" sequence. If she is progressing from one general stage to the next, then she's doing what's normal for her.

What *should* you do to help your baby develop in a healthy way? We think the first thing is to banish the notion that earlier is better. Throw out the "schedule" and stop comparing her to other babies. Take the pressure to perform off your child (and off yourself).

Let your baby progress at the rate which pleases her. This way every one of her accomplishments will contribute to her self-esteem in the most positive way possible.

We also suggest that you change your focus from the gross motor skills, like sitting and walking, to the fine ones, like grasping and eye tracking. If you pay more attention to these little details of her development, you'll discover that something is happening literally every day. You'll also get to enjoy the studied concentration she applies to each new skill.

By tuning in to the smaller, more subtle abilities she is developing, you'll have a much better understanding of how your baby functions and learns.

REACHING AND GRASPING

As any mother knows, babies begin to exercise their arms and legs from the middle of pregnancy. At birth your baby actually can reach in a wobbly fashion, but newborn infants generally are not given much opportunity to reach for objects.

The mobiles and stuffed animals that surround their cribs are usually placed outside their limited field of vision and objects that do come into view don't ordinarily stay there long enough for the infants to organize their movements.

Hold a ball *close* above your newborn's face for several minutes when she is alert and quiet, and she may well reach out and swat it. Her reach is very slow and clumsy, though, so even if she does manage to grasp the ball momentarily, she won't have the strength or coordination to hold onto it.

No one knows whether this early form of reaching is intentional or reflexive, or whether it could be sustained and strengthened with consistent practice. The fact is, in most infants it disappears at about four weeks and does not recur until about four months. At that point, the infant becomes much more intent on her game and begins to polish it into a viable skill.

As she refines her reach, your child develops the coordination needed to aim, launch and reach, and to adjust the direction if she is off course. Instead of randomly opening and closing her fist, she waits to open her hand widely until she sees the hand is near the target, and she won't close her fingers around an object until she can actually feel it.

In this way, she separates the motion of reaching from grasping. To improve her odds even further, she soon starts reaching with two hands, using one hand to locate the object while the other tries to grasp it.

Developmentalist T. G. R. Bower used a simple method to help infants learn mature reaching skills: each day he dangled a small toy above the crib, teasing the baby to reach for it. He chose to dangle the object because its motion forced the child to concentrate on the location of the target and to feel for it before grasping. It also encouraged the use of two hands. The babies in this study learned to reach and grasp several weeks earlier than a control group who did not have target practice.

D I S C O V E R Y   P L A Y

Reaching and Grasping

Play a similar discovery game with your own infant. (We remind you again—these games are not meant to speed the baby's learning, but to alert you to some subtle, but important, skills that are developing.) Starting when she is about three months old, use a ribbon to suspend a small rattle or high-contrast toy from a bar or similar support over the baby's crib, play yard or infant seat so the target is just within her reach. Never leave the side of the crib during these play sessions or your baby could become entangled in the ribbon. If you must leave in the middle of a session, remove the dangling object before you leave your baby alone.

You may want to wiggle the toy at first to attract your baby's attention, but then stand back out of her sight and let her respond as she chooses. If she makes

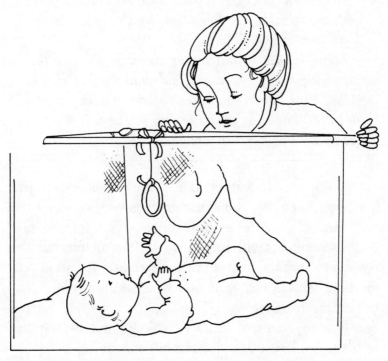

Encourage your baby to reach and grasp by suspending a ring or rattle so that it is just within her reach. Remove the object before leaving the baby alone, and if you use a suspension apparatus across the crib, remove it entirely by five months or before she learns to sit alone.

no motion toward the object, it probably means she's not yet ready for this game. Wait a week or two and then try again. If she does bat at the object, then your timing is right.

Let her play for five or ten minutes a session, removing the object before she gets bored. If she manages to grab the object and does not let go, take it from her, to keep the ribbon and support from breaking loose and falling into the crib. If she wants to play with the freed toy at this point, by all means let her. She's earned it.

Many babies would rather continue the swatting game, however. Let your child guide you. (NOTE: When your baby is able to sit alone, remove all bars and toys that hang over the crib so she will not pull them down or become entangled.)

One way to help your child discover her hands is to give her brightly colored fingerless mittens or socks with the ends cut off. According to Dr. Burton White, who first used such mittens with infants two to four months old, the color and motion help attract the child's attention and promote hand-eye coordination, which is essential for controlled reaching later on. You might want to repeat the dangling toy experiment with colored mittens on her hands to see how this influences her actions.

SITTING UP

As you play with your baby in the first days after birth it may be hard to believe she will ever have the strength to sit up by herself, let alone stand and walk. Pull her up slightly by the hands, and her head will flop backward like a rag doll's. At this point in life, she barely has the strength to stretch her legs out straight. This situation changes very gradually.

It usually takes several weeks for a baby to develop enough neck strength to hold her head up without support. It takes months before she'll be able to keep her head erect and steady for more than ten minutes. The best way to help your baby strengthen her muscles during the first weeks is to change her position frequently.

Most infants get bored and fussy if they lie down too long and will let you know they need to be moved, but you should try to be alert to this before your baby complains. She probably won't be able to roll over on her own until her fourth or fifth month, so you should do it for her frequently, from her stomach to her back and from side to side.

Take her in your arms and rock her. Hold her in your lap and gently swing her arms and legs.

Introduce her slowly to the sitting position by placing her in an infant seat for a few minutes at a time. It will probably take about three months before she can sit in such a seat for thirty minutes on her own. Once she is able to, let her start sitting up in her stroller or a swing. (Make sure she's securely strapped in every time.)

After she's comfortable sitting up with support, she will probably start to experiment with sitting on her own (usually between six and eight months). As her back strengthens and her reach becomes more mature, she will learn to use her arms to keep herself upright. In a matter of a few months her hands will be free to explore while her back alone supports her.

Every baby has her own preferred technique for getting to a sitting position. Some children learn to sit down from a crawling position. Some wait until they can stand before discovering a way to sit down. Squatting, stooping, plopping and pulling are all perfectly legitimate approaches to sitting. Your baby will experiment to find the methods that work best for her.

CREEPING AND CRAWLING

Once your baby has the knack of sitting on her own, usually between six and nine months, she'll start working on locomotion. Few activities are more appealing to an eight-month-old than moving across the floor. The preparation for independent movement begins long before your baby can actually crawl.

Infants seem intuitively to know which muscles they need to strengthen to perform specific motor activities. They also seem to know that exercise is the best way to get these muscles in shape. You'll see your baby lying on her back and kicking in the air. This is how she tones her legs and feet for crawling and walking. She doesn't need to be trained to kick and wiggle, but there are ways you can make this exercise more fun for her. Try tying bells to her ankles or toes, so that each kick rewards her with a sound, or suspend an inflated ball or rattle within reach of her feet so she can kick it and make it move.

When your baby is ready, she naturally will begin making more advances toward walking. The day she rolls over, you'll know she's on her way. From this point on, she will develop her own distinctive methods of getting around. These methods vary widely from one child to the next, but the following patterns are among the most common:

- *Creeping.* The child lies on her belly and pushes herself forward or backward with her arms while steering with her feet. Many babies creep before they can crawl, and most start out going backward only. This is because, in the early months, the muscles needed to push backward are stronger than the muscles needed to pull forward.
- *Crawling.* The baby gets up on her hands or elbows and knees, holding her belly up off the floor. This requires a good deal more strength in the arms, legs and back muscles than does creeping.
- *Hurtling.* From a crouch position on hands and knees, the infant throws herself forward while flinging her limbs outward. This may look painful to you, but you shouldn't interfere unless your child is likely to fall on an object that could harm her.
- *Bottoming.* While sitting up, the baby propels herself forward or backward with her arms and legs. This works best on a smooth floor, which allows her to slide.

While a few infants bypass these preliminary phases and walk before they crawl, most use many different methods of locomotion before they finally achieve upright movement. This trial-and-error process helps them exercise different muscle groups and develop overall coordination.

There is no reason to rush a baby past this stage to

walking. The best way to help your child is to clear your floor of obstacles and dangerous objects so she can travel in whatever fashion she prefers.

Try not to carry her about the house unless she insists. It may test your patience to wait as she slowly propels herself across the room, but the message you're sending her is a valuable one: she is a strong and capable individual in her own right. *This* is the message that will bring out the best in your baby.

UP AND WALKING

Walking, like reaching, develops in stages. If you hold your newborn up soon after birth so the soles of her feet touch the floor or tabletop, she will take "steps" as if marching. Under ordinary circumstances, however, this reflex newborn "walking" response disappears by about the eighth week.

Months later, the baby starts over from scratch, learning first to creep or crawl and then, when the muscles of her neck, back, hips and legs are strong enough, to stand and walk independently.

Your baby will let you know that she's ready to stand by bouncing, stepping in place or watching her feet as you hold her up by the arms. As she sits in her crib or playpen she will plant her feet, bend her legs and grab for the sides to support herself. Eventually she will learn to pull herself all the way up hand over hand, as if climbing a rope.

The first time your baby manages to pull herself to a full standing position she may act surprised and scared. Like a cat up a tree, she probably won't know how to get down, and she'll cry for help. You'll sit her down and, immediately, she will be on her feet again.

Her desire to get up and walk is so great that no amount of frustration can stop her. When she gets used to standing it may be almost impossible to persuade her to sit or lie down. We've even heard of babies falling asleep while standing up! As demanding as this may be on you, try to indulge her, because there is no better way for her to learn. At any rate, have faith. It won't take long for her to learn how to get down by herself. Help her a few times with the maneuver, and she may learn more quickly to do it by herself.

At this stage, your most important concern should be safety. Make sure she has access to large secure objects, such as furniture that won't slide, or you, to use for support. Get rid of all breakable objects and obstacles, and unstable supports like tablecloths, lamps and low-hanging objects that she might be tempted to use in pulling herself up to a standing position.

· The next step toward walking is learning to stand without support. It may take her several more months and hundreds of falls before your baby learns this maneuver. She'll probably start by "cruising" alongside a steady support such as a sofa or table, or she may take her first steps while you hold her hands.

Gradually she will learn to walk using just one of your hands for support. Eventually she'll let go and use her hands freely for balance, like a tightrope walker, with arms held high and wide. Bit by bit, her skills and confidence will increase until she can stop, turn around, back up and bend down. The pièce de résistance comes when she man-

ages to hold a toy in her hands while marching trium-
phantly across the room.

Don't try to rush this process. Wait until she starts
"cruising" on her own. Then you can offer your hands for
support. (This is one activity that siblings love to share
with their baby brothers and sisters.) You also may want
to rearrange the furniture so it is easier for her to reach as
she moves around the room.

We don't recommend using a "walker." These wheeled
seats can actually inhibit the development of walking because they dissuade babies from crawling and standing. In
order to move about in a walker, the baby utilizes the
lower leg muscles, instead of the thigh muscles she needs
for walking independently. Also, walkers give the baby a
false sense of confidence that can lead to accidents.

More than three thousand babies are injured each year
when their walkers tip over or fall down stairs. A walker
can make your life unnecessarily hectic as well, since it
allows your baby to move much faster than she would on
her own. As a rule of thumb, when considering any piece
of "training equipment," ask yourself how it really con-
tributes to the learning process. If it only serves as a
crutch, don't use it.

Once your baby begins to navigate securely on her own,
you may want to equip her with push-pull toys that give
her a sense of being supported without actually providing
support. The toys that squeak, pop or twirl as they move
also provide your baby with an extra incentive to walk
about.

A good way to enhance her walking pleasure (and
yours) is to take excursions together to the park, beach or
even just around the block. Keep the distances short and

give yourselves plenty of time so your baby will have ample opportunity to explore new sights and sounds without getting fatigued.

COORDINATING MOTOR SKILLS

Once your baby has crossed the major hurdles of learning to reach, grasp, stand and walk, she will begin refining and integrating her movements. Gradually she will learn to use her hands, to catch and throw, to use crayons and pencils and to manipulate her hands independently of each other. This process will continue all the way to adulthood.

D I S C O V E R Y   P L A Y

Coordination

Although you may be tempted to buy fancy "child development toys," you will soon find that ordinary household objects work just as well for helping babies discover their fledgling talents. Here are some suggestions for supplies and activities that can help you make physical maturation fun.

- *Paper and Fabric. When your baby is just beginning to manipulate her hands, her favorite "toys" may be stiff pieces of fabric and paper. Try to find brightly colored and patterned fabrics such as denim, linen or heavy cotton. Cut them into one-foot squares and let your baby* discover all the ways these squares react as she grabs and bunches them together.

Another favorite with babies at about five months is crackly paper, like the paper dry cleaners wrap around shirts. We also recommend giving your baby an old magazine (one you no longer care about!) every now and then. She'll pull, wrinkle and tear the paper to shreds with great delight. These experiences teach her far better than any store-bought toy the kind of power she has—literally—at her fingertips.

- *Ball Play.* Keep a large, lightweight ball, such as a beach ball, available for two- or three-person games. Show your child how to move the ball using different parts of her body, including elbows, knees and head as well as hands and feet. Create a "goal" by turning a wastebasket or box on its side and rolling the ball into the box. As your baby becomes more skillful, toss the ball to her and encourage her to throw it either to you or into the "goal."

  Use the ball, also, as a piece of "gym" equipment, lying your baby on top of it and rolling her slowly back and forth. She'll laugh with glee as she works to maintain her balance. The activity will help her develop balance and coordination while strengthening many of her muscles.

- *Container Play.* Your baby will learn to develop fine hand coordination by using containers in filling, pouring and stacking games. Search your house for containers of all shapes and sizes, including plastic bottles, wooden boxes, metal bowls and paper envelopes that are safe for your baby to use this way.

You'll want containers on hand outside for sand and dirt play, in the tub for water play, and in the kitchen so your little one can "help" you as you prepare meals. Try to find containers that fit inside each other, so she can explore relationships of shape and size as she plays.

• *Beads, Blocks, Puzzles.* When you shop for toys, look for activity-oriented items that help your baby with eye-hand coordination and dexterity. Building toys, such as blocks and interlocking shapes, are good for this purpose. So are beads she can string (they must be large enough so they can't be swallowed), pegs she can hammer into a block, shape sorters, stacking sets and simplified jigsaw puzzles.

All of these toys are available in inexpensive models. Remember, the price tag is no guarantee of educational value.

• *Music.* The rhythm and motion of music encourages your baby to use her body in many different ways. In the process, she will develop balance, posture and improved coordination. Set aside a special time each day to play or dance with music.

Initially, you'll have to carry her in your arms while doing this. Before long, she'll be doing her own fancy steps alongside you. Vary the selections to create different moods and pacing. Supply your baby with some "instruments" that allow her to make "music" herself.

Instruments such as drums, xylophones, tambourines, pianos and castanets make ideal first instruments, because they add opportunities to develop manual dexterity. If you don't have adult versions of these instruments around the house (or if they are too valuable), invest in the inexpensive infant models.

- *Furniture.* If given the opportunity, your little one will utilize every piece of furniture in the house as a plaything. Soft furniture is an irresistible target for jumping and bouncing, while rockers provide a wonderful means of calming down after a period of high activity. (Make sure your rocker is weighted so that it can't tip over if your baby gets too energetic.)

She'll push light chairs about the house as she learns to walk. She will remove the pillows from your sofa and explore all the different ways she can stack them. Your life will be calmer if you just resign yourself to the fact that your furniture is going to get rough treatment for the next fifteen years.

If you have some pieces that are too valuable for that kind of attitude, give your child and yourself a break by making them impossible to get to, but try to keep those items to a minimum so she won't be overly restricted and frustrated.

The best way to help bring out your baby's motor skills is to stand back and let her go. Applaud her successes and provide encouragement for her to try again when she fails. Respond when she asks for assistance, but don't hover in her shadow or pressure her to "perform" (even when relatives or friends are visiting).

Your baby doesn't really need you to teach her how to manipulate her body. She is innately programmed to do it herself. But you can help make it a more joyful process. Physical activity can be a wonderful way to learn about each other, enrich your relationship and have fun together.

· XI ·

Thinking
and Knowing:
The Cognitive
Processes

Every day your baby is experimenting with the world around her. Her tests of cause and effect help her to make judgments about the way things work. She becomes increasingly aware of her relationship to her surroundings and, in time, begins to think like an adult. This process, which will continue for the rest of her life, is called cognitive development.

In the beginning, your baby will focus on the people and objects around her. Who and what are they? How do they work? How do they relate to her? How can she affect them?

Soon her attention will turn to language and communication. What are others trying to tell her? How can *she* express her thoughts and feelings to the people around her? She will also start to explore more abstract mysteries, such as numerical concepts, and she'll begin working out her theories about the world through various types of fantasy play.

Each of these cognitive areas is essential to your child's intellectual growth. Each will unfold according to her unique pattern and timetable. You can give her the tools she needs to explore and experiment, but don't push her to use them before she is ready. You cannot force her to be interested in a subject or task simply because it interests you.

Your baby will let you know when she is ready to take on a new problem, and she will make it clear what kinds of challenges interest her. She will eagerly attack them on her own, struggle determinedly to overcome them and beam with pleasure when she reaches a solution. Unlike some older children and adults, babies need no special encouragement to learn. *Unless a grownup spoils the process, babies think that learning is play.*

Infant researcher Hanus Papousek created a game to test babies' enthusiasm for intellectual challenges. He devised a special infant chair that allowed babies to control light switches simply by moving their heads to the right or left. These switches were connected to a small light display positioned directly in front of the chair.

At first the babies would wriggle randomly, trying to figure out how the lights worked. Once they had learned the secret, they would grow quiet. But if the system was changed, so they had to turn their heads in the other direction to turn on the light, they started to grin and again become active. When they mastered the second system, they again calmed down and lost interest.

The babies in Papousek's experiment were given no special rewards for their efforts, and even the flashing of the light was of minor interest to them, since they barely looked at it. Their sole motivation seemed to come from the challenge and delight of learning the system. That was enough to keep them actively involved.

SOLVING PROBLEMS

If you spend much time watching your baby explore her surroundings, you know there is both method and intensity to her play. Few of her movements are random; most reflect very specific intentions and interests. At times she will become so immersed in her activity that she ignores everything else around her.

Often, she will work so hard that she grunts or groans in exertion. Her ultimate goal, whether she consciously knows it or not, is to develop or refine a new skill or ability. If left to her own devices she will persist until she's achieved that goal. Developmental psychologist Dr. Jerome Bruner believes this process consists of three phases:

1. *Intention.* Your baby makes the decision to take on a new challenge. Perhaps she's seen a toy she wants to

hold or an obstacle she wants to climb. Once she has established the intention, she will experiment with all sorts of maneuvers to reach her goal. As soon as she loses that desire, she will stop working.

2. *Trial and Error.* Your baby plays with all the variables involved in the task at hand. If she has decided to make a noise with a drum, she may kick it with her foot, bang it with her hand or throw it on the floor. Eventually, she might throw a stick or a block on the drum to see what sound that makes.

3. *Refinement.* Once she has figured out the basic means to her desired end, your infant will begin tailoring her activity for style and efficiency. She will practice the way she holds a crayon between her fingers or the way she pushes her rolling toy. She will explore novel ways of applying her new skills and begin playing with them simply for the fun of it.

Not all babies attack problems with the same level of intensity. Researchers have found that one-year-olds faced with a standard problem (getting around a barrier in order to reach a toy) will respond in one of three ways:

· The most successful problem-solvers work intently and persistently, without becoming upset, until they manage to reach their goal.
· A less determined group gives up as soon as it recognizes the challenge, and is easily distracted.
· The third group is reduced to tears by the challenge and refuses either to make an effort to solve the problem or to become engaged in another activity.

UNDERSTANDING OBJECTS

The first learning challenges confronting your baby all involve objects and space. By objects we mean people and animals as well as things. In the beginning, your baby cannot distinguish the traits that separate living from nonliving creatures. This is just one of the cognitive hurdles she will make during her first year.

Another challenge is learning to identify objects by their physical traits and spatial characteristics. As adults, we take it for granted that objects can either rest in one place or travel through space. We assume that objects on wheels can roll across the ground, that some objects float while others sink.

Without looking, we know how to adjust the level of a cup or glass, depending on the amount of liquid it contains, so we can drink without spilling. But we once had to learn these concepts by watching and thinking, just as your baby is doing in the first months of her life.

Psychologists believe that young infants do, in fact, begin with certain assumptions about the way objects function in space, but these assumptions are bizarre by adult standards. Newborns, it seems, identify objects not by how they look, but by how they behave and where they are located.

An object that is not located within the infant's view does not exist for her. If an object changes location, it becomes an entirely different object. For example, when your baby sees her teddy bear in the crib, she does not recognize it as the same teddy bear that sits with her in her playpen or as the bear that her brother waves over her head from time to time in play. Although these are in fact the same bear, she sees them as three different toys: the crib bear, the playpen bear and the moving bear.

This means your child's intellectual universe is populated by thousands of objects more than are actually there. One function of her developing cognitive awareness is to help her simplify this view of her surroundings. She will ultimately understand that while some things (toys, people, cars) tend to move more than others (sky, trees, houses, walls), everything can either move or remain in one position.

Gradually she discovers that every object has certain variable qualities, which include location and movements through space. By the middle of her first year she starts to realize that objects continue to exist after they move out of sight.

You may be surprised, and perhaps a bit unnerved, to learn that your baby probably views you in the same way as other objects during her first few months. That is, she believes there are many different versions of you, one in each part of the house.

Researchers have tested this notion with babies younger and older than five months. The babies were confronted by three simultaneous images of their mothers presented by means of a trick screen. The babies younger than five months seemed delighted to see three mothers at once and smiled at each image individually. The babies older than five months, on the other hand, became distraught at the idea that their mothers could appear in three different places at once.

Apparently, at some point around the fifth month, each child comes to the conclusion that he has one and only one mother and will protest any evidence to the contrary.

It's at this point that babies begin to cry when their parents leave them, because they now comprehend that the parent who disappears may not automatically come back. From here on out, your child's trust in you is based on experience rather than assumption.

D I S C O V E R Y P L A Y

Object Perception

You can use Discovery Play to find out how your baby perceives objects. Repeat these games at regular intervals, and you will be able to observe her changing understanding of things in the world around her.

Beginning when she is about three months old, show her how a toy train works by moving it back and forth across the floor. First move it to the right, then left, then right again. She'll probably follow the movement easily and will decide that this is the train that moves back and forth.

But what happens if, after awhile, you move the train a different way—this time from right to left, then farther left again? Your baby may look back to the right, expecting the train to continue on course even though you moved it in the opposite direction before her very eyes. Moreover, once the train comes to a full stop, she may search back along its course for a moving version of a train.

No matter how obvious it may seem to you, your

baby may not see that the trains which moved in different directions around her were always the same train.

You can also explore your baby's understanding of this concept by abruptly removing or changing objects in her environment. Place a doll directly in front of her for a few seconds, then—without warning—replace it with a bucket and observe her reaction. Blow a soap bubble in front of her and see what she does when it bursts.

In the first few months she will accept these events as being perfectly ordinary. Later in the year, after she develops what scientists call the "object concept," she will either protest or search for the vanished toy or bubble.

Once she realizes that each object in her world is unique, the next conceptual task facing your baby is to figure out how objects relate to one another in space. What does it mean to be "next to," "on top of" or "underneath"? Is an object that's on top of a block separate from the block or is it part of the block? These are difficult questions for an infant. It may take months of experimentation before she can answer them with confidence.

Her experimentation consists of playing with objects and exploring all the different ways they connect. In the beginning, your infant assumes that objects which share a common boundary are both part of one large object. If a cup sits on a cloth, she will probably pull on the cloth to bring the cup closer. If the cup sits next to the edge of the cloth, she will still pull the cloth expecting to bring the cup toward her. Most children don't fully understand the difference between these two situations until they are about ten months old.

Object Relationships

Another difficult concept involves the notion that one object can exist on top of another one and yet remain separate. Put a block on top of a box. Your three- to five-month-old baby will treat the block and the box as a single object. She may accidentally knock the block off, but she does not understand that the two are separate to begin with. In the latter half of the year she will learn that she can shake the block free when it's on that particular box.

But if you then place the block on a different box, she will continue to shake the first box. In her mind, it's the action of shaking that box which produces her block. She doesn't understand the spatial relationships between objects, nor does she see that these relationships operate the same way no matter which objects are used.

Much the same thing happens when you drop a ball in a cup (even a transparent cup). After the first few demonstrations with one cup, your baby will discover that she can retrieve the ball after you drop it. If you then drop the ball into a second cup, she will still search for it in the first one. It's as though she believes the ball belongs to the first cup and no other.

Babies get most of these spatial relationships straight by the tenth or eleventh month. The confusion remains, however, when you start shifting the positions of the objects around. For example, take two cups and place them in front of your baby. Drop a ball in the cup to her right and then switch the cups so the ball is now on her left. She will continue to look for the ball in the right-hand cup.

The same thing happens if, instead of moving the cups, you move your baby, so the cups appear to be in different positions. It's as if babies younger than eighteen months assume that their perspective is the only correct perspective. They just don't understand that they must adjust their bearings as they move around and as objects move around them.

You can help your baby sort out these difficult concepts by doing things during Discovery Play that give her a small advantage. If, for example, you are playing a game of hide-the-ball (placing a ball behind one of two or three barriers), don't delay before asking your baby to start searching. The shorter the time she must remember the ball's location, the less likely she is to forget it.

You might also use a more attractive object as the focus of your game. An interesting doll or stuffed animal, particularly one your child has never seen before, may prove easier for your baby to track than a simple block or ball. This encourages her to pay attention, a crucial part of succeeding in this kind of activity. Remember, the purpose of these games is discovery. The goal is success, not frustration.

UNDERSTANDING LIQUIDS

Most babies are fascinated with liquids. Few activities make them as happy as splashing or pouring water, turning faucets on and off and playing under the sprinkler. Liquids are not like any other objects, and yet they can be stored in and emptied from the very same containers that hold balls and blocks. Many of them are also good to drink, which makes them particularly attractive to infants. That's why you must never leave toxic liquids anywhere your baby can get near them.

Your infant begins to study the properties of water with her first bath, but the real challenge comes when she is confronted with the problem of drinking from a cup. All at once, she must account for the laws of gravity, the physical properties of liquids, and the effect of the shape and angle of the cup on the flow of the liquid inside. It's not surprising that it takes her awhile to catch on.

The first time most babies confront a cup (usually around six months), they simply turn it upside down as if they expect the liquid to fall out like a solid object. When the contents splash all over them, they are either delighted or dismayed, depending on how thirsty they are. Your baby will probably figure out the problem well enough to be drinking from a cup quite smoothly by her first birthday.

If you switch containers, however, she may have some difficulty. Pour her milk from a narrow cup into a wide cup, for example, and she will tip the second cup to the same angle she was using with the first. To her surprise, she won't be able to reach the milk. If the switch is from wide to narrow, she'll tip the new cup too far, drenching herself in the process.

Try these activities with your baby, but use water in the cup and do it outside or during her bath so you won't be distressed by her spills. Not until she's about fifteen months old will she conquer all the practical problems related to liquids, containers and drinking.

UNDERSTANDING QUANTITY

When you look at a cluster of seven beans and another of five beans, you know without actually counting that the cluster of seven has more beans. A baby, however, decides which group is larger not on the basis of how many components it contains, but rather on the shape of the cluster. If five beans are spread out in a long line and seven beans are clumped together in a short line, your one-year-old probably will assume that the long line of five has more beans. If the five beans are spread out too much, however, she may choose the more densely packed grouping.

Not until she's about eighteen months old will she consistently pick the correct group when asked which has the most or the least. By this point, she has learned to rely not just on the appearance of the arrangement, but on the actual one-to-one correspondences between the elements in the two groups. Even though she most likely will be five or six before she can answer such problems verbally, she will show you that she can "count out" before she's two.

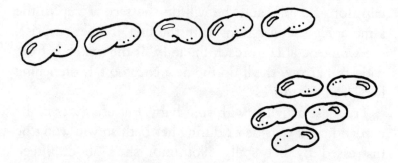

Though there are five beans in both of these clusters, your baby probably sees the long line of beans as having "more" than the dense cluster.

D I S C O V E R Y   P L A Y

Volume and Weight

Your baby goes through the same learning process as she grapples with issues of volume. Hand your one-year-old a long, thin rod, and she will tense her muscles preparing for a heavy burden. Hand her a short, fat block, and she'll be surprised by its heavy weight. Take a long, thin container full of juice, pour it into a short, wide glass and then ask your daughter which container has more. She'll probably point to the long container. She judges relative volume just as she does quantity, by the way things look. She does not yet realize that the volume is exactly the same, regardless of the shape of the container.

You can help your baby learn about her world by giving her as many opportunities as possible to explore relationships between different sizes, amounts, and numbers of objects and liquids. As you go through your everyday activities, help her work through problems of relative size (which is larger, fewer, heavier). Whenever you can, use numbers to describe objects (one cucumber and three carrots).

It will be many more months before your child can use numerals or make specific mathematical calculations. However, by learning the general principles of quantity and volume now, she is laying the essential groundwork for the mathematical and scientific lessons to come.

THE BEGINNINGS OF LANGUAGE AND SPEECH

One of the greatest triumphs of early childhood is the development of language and speech. The ability to talk not only gives your child a means of communicating with others, but also provides her with an essential tool for abstract reasoning.

Labeling objects gives your baby a way to hold those objects in mind, even when they're out of sight. This, coupled with the discovery that objects do, in fact, continue to exist when they are out of sight, makes it possible for her to use her imagination and creativity, solve extended mental problems, and compare the past and present.

Most linguists believe that babies essentially teach themselves to talk. There is little anyone can do to speed up the rate of this learning, although families can inhibit a child's willingness to speak. Children raised in active, highly vocal homes tend to be more talkative. Babies raised in extremely quiet homes, or by parents who discourage them from talking, tend to be more taciturn.

But this is not to say that quiet babies understand language any less than chatty infants. Many children withhold conversation for emotional reasons long after they have actually learned how to talk.

Your baby will begin experimenting with speech during her first month. She listens to the sounds you make when you talk to her, and she responds with little throaty sounds. Some of her first real attempts at verbal communication may be cries of hunger or discomfort.

You can teach her that her sounds are important by responding promptly to these messages, encouraging her to make noise and send you other signals through the movement of her body. Over the next few months she will progress in spurts, first learning to babble a variety of syllables, then clarifying her pronunciation and finally, before the end of the first year, combining these sounds into a few real words. In the process, she will begin to imitate adult intonations, and her babbling will actually start to take on the sound of sentences, questions and exclamations.

The first words your baby learns are nouns, the names of the objects and people around her. Not surprisingly, she concentrates on objects that she can manipulate actively or which hold particular interest for her. She will be much less interested in naming things she cannot control. This is one reason why you should try to give your child access to as large a variety as possible of stimulating objects and toys.

Branching out from nouns, your baby will start to learn adjectives and verbs that help her track what she's doing, what's happening around her and how she feels. "Hungry," "thirsty," "more," "all gone," "bye-bye" and "go" are examples of these early action words, all of them having an immediate meaning to your baby.

As a rule, your baby understands the meaning of a given word several months before she can pronounce it. That's why it's important for you to talk to your infant from the first days of life. Even though she cannot return your conversation, introduce her to the many individual sounds that make up words. Use clear, simple language—not baby talk.

As you change her and feed her, tell her what you're doing. Name all the toys in her nursery, and talk to her about their colors, textures and shapes. When you're walking with her, point out interesting objects or sights around you. At first it may be difficult to conduct these one-way conversations without feeling a little silly. Once your baby begins to smile, you'll see how much she enjoys it. Before long, her active babbling will give the two of you a way to "talk" to each other.

D I S C O V E R Y   P L A Y

Language

Reading and singing are especially important for helping your baby develop her language skills. It's never too early to introduce her to the process of reading, though you'll want to limit your reading sessions to no more than fifteen minutes at a stretch during the first few months.

Never force reading sessions on your baby if she's fidgety or upset. Try to find a time of day when she is quiet and attentive.

Start out with very short stories or poems with a regular cadence. Babies love rhythmic poems such as nursery rhymes, the experts say, because the rhythm reminds them of their mother's heartbeat. Lullabies and other songs have the same soothing effect.

Don't worry about the quality of your voice. Your baby will enjoy the music in either case. In no time you'll find certain songs that are clearly her favorites. Use these songs to calm her down when she's crying and cheer her up when she's moody.

After the first couple of months, when your baby's range of vision starts to expand, point out the pictures in her storybooks to her. Look for illustrations that have bold colors, high in contrast. Make sure there are lots of figures with full faces, as opposed to pro-files. It seems that babies have a hard time identifying profiles, since they are used to dealing with people in a face-to-face manner.

Talk about the stories with your child as you read. If the text mentions water or sky, let her know that these are like the water in her bath and the sky she sees out the window. In the same way, use books as a source of conversation about abstract concepts, like numbers, geometric forms and relationships between objects. When you come across phrases like "on top of," "more than," "round" or "square," use the objects in her room to show her what these phrases mean.

As your baby's reach and grasp develop, make sure she gets a chance to handle her books herself. Surround her with books made of cloth, unbreakable board or vinyl (the bath is a great place to "read" vinyl books). Give her your old magazines when you've finished reading them (but only if you're willing to see them torn up). Let her play occasionally with "real" books.

Many babies love to rearrange the books on bookshelves and exchange them with you in play. These games help build your baby's familiarity and love of books, which will eventually increase her enthusiasm for reading on her own.

These early months are also a good time to introduce your baby to other languages, so she becomes familiar with the variety of sounds involved. If someone in the family speaks a second language, make an effort to use it with your baby, but try not to mix the two languages. The baby is less likely to become confused if she hears the second language exclusively from one person. If no one is fluent enough to talk in the foreign language all the time, try setting aside a particular time each day to talk to the baby in the second language. Read to her from children's books or play records with children's songs in that language. Avoid switching languages in mid-sentence or throwing foreign words into the mix at random. This can confuse the child and may make it more difficult for her to learn either language properly.

During the second year your toddler will begin to play with words on her own. At first she will use one or two words to represent whole sentences. "Book," for example, may mean "Bring me that book" or "Read the book" or "Take this book." Gradually she will learn to change her inflection to let you know which meaning applies.

She will also start to combine nouns with adjectives and verbs to extend the length and complexity of her sentences. At times she is bound to mispronounce words, but don't correct her. Instead, try to use the word correctly yourself in a sentence, pronouncing it clearly and properly. After a few repetitions your toddler will adopt the correct pronunciation.

LANGUAGE PROBLEMS

By the end of the second year most children have a vocabulary of up to one hundred words and are capable of constructing two-word sentences. Some children encounter setbacks, however, which disrupt their progress. The most common problems are delayed speech, pronunciation difficulties and stuttering. Generally these are temporary hurdles, but they can be disturbing to you as a parent. It may help you to understand what causes them and how you can help your child get past them.

The term "delayed speech" is used to describe the problem when a child's speech is unintelligible, when her vocabulary is much smaller than is normal for her age or when she fails to talk at all. There are six possible reasons for delayed speech, including both physiological and psychological causes:

1. The child doesn't feel the need to communicate. Most babies discover the power of language during the second six months as they consciously begin to use cries and gestures to get their families to respond to them. If the family somehow predicts and provides for a child's every wish ahead of time, she may not see the use of speaking and may, effectively, choose to remain mute. It's not a question of "spoiling" the child, but rather a case of overdoing things for her.

2. The child is experiencing some sort of emotional conflict. If a baby feels somehow afraid or unwilling to express herself, she may not learn to talk. She may see this as a kind of protection. As a parent, you'll want to encourage your child to participate in conversations. Show an interest in her sounds and gestures. Let her know that you value what she has to contribute.

3. The baby may have some physical disability that interferes with speech. If your baby has trouble breathing, opening or closing her vocal cords, moving her jaw or tongue, she will probably have difficulty talking. Check with the infant's doctor to be sure that none of these is the problem.

4. The delay may be the result of a mental disorder. Language requires that the child be able to process information and translate it into verbal symbols. Certain kinds of brain injuries produce a condition called aphasia, which can interrupt this process, causing the child to confuse or lose words for thoughts. A child may be extremely bright and still be aphasic.

5. The child may have trouble hearing. Normal hearing is essential for the proper development of language skills. This is one reason why your baby's hearing should be checked by her doctor in the first months of life.

6. Mental and/or physical retardation may interfere with the ability to speak.

Pronunciation difficulties may be hard to detect before the child is three or four. It's perfectly normal for younger children to babble unintelligibly as they practice making various sounds. They also tend to replace difficult sounds with sounds that are easy to pronounce.

This is why little children tend to say "wed" and "lellow" instead of "red" and "yellow." Don't try to correct these early mistakes directly. Just make sure you always pronounce the words correctly in your own speech.

When a child does not outgrow her early language mistakes, she may develop a speech impediment. Any of the following could be the cause:

1. The child may have started talking later than usual, or may have experienced an illness that set her back. These developmental delays will not cause any permanent damage.

2. The child may be confusing sounds from different languages. If yours is a bilingual household, make sure the child's exposure to the different languages does not overlap. While the confusion of two languages will not cause permanent problems, the child will have an easier time if she is clearly able to differentiate one from the other.

3. The family may be discouraging the child from learning to speak or providing a poor speech model. If you routinely use baby talk when addressing your child, or if

you reinforce her mistakes by repeating them back to her, she will have a hard time learning the correct way to speak.

If a child feels she's being neglected or unloved, she may misspeak on purpose in order to get attention. If she is left for long periods with baby-sitters who don't speak correctly, she may imitate their speech patterns.

4. The child's mispronunciation may be caused by an abnormality of the jaw, tongue, lips, teeth or palate. The earlier such physical abnormalities are identified and treated, the less they will interfere with the child's development of normal speech.

Stuttering occurs in up to 5 percent of children between the ages of two and four years. In some children it involves the uncontrollable repetition of consonant or vowel sounds. In others it involves the repetition of whole words or phrases. Usually, stuttering disappears naturally after a few months.

The best way to help a child overcome stuttering is to ignore it and eliminate any factors that might be contributing to it. The most common causes for stuttering include the following:

1. The child feels pressured to talk before she is ready.
2. The child is tense or frightened. Stuttering may be a nervous reaction, like stage fright. Stuttering often occurs when children are exposed to a new environment or a group of strangers. It is exacerbated when the mother is tense or when the child is strictly disciplined. Pressure to learn too many new skills at once can also contribute to stuttering.
3. If a child is forced to switch from being left-handed to right-handed, she might develop stuttering. This is be-

cause right- or left-handedness and speech are both controlled by the same part of the brain. Interference with one process can have a negative impact on the other as well.

Developing speech will be one of the greatest triumphs of your child's early years. As she develops the skill of communicating verbally, she will become increasingly eager to share her thoughts and discoveries with you (and anyone else who will listen). Even though this steady stream of chatter may be exhausting for you, encourage her to keep it up.

Make sure she receives the kind of stimulation that gives her topics for conversation. Ask her questions and listen to her answers. Point out the sounds that come from other sources: the *tick-tock* of the clock, the *beep* of the horn, the *cheep* of the birds outside the window. Make a game of naming objects and activities as you play together.

Include your baby in family conversations, even if it means silencing everyone else from time to time so she has an opportunity to speak. This is the only way she will learn to use language to piece together the thousands of new ideas that confront her every day.

FANTASY PLAY

As your baby gets older she will begin to incorporate all her skills into fantasy play. The world of make-believe allows her to explore applications of those skills that might be impossible for her to try out in real life. She will pretend to draw a magnificent painting, for example, or play an instrument in an orchestra.

In this way, fantasy play is important in helping little children find out which skills and interests are meaningful to them and which they want to pursue as they get older. Fantasy play also helps young children develop creativity and resourcefulness.

Most of us think of make-believe as the elaborate games of "let's pretend" we remember from our own childhoods. That level of fantasy play begins at around age three. But soon after your baby moves into her second year she will begin to use a less sophisticated form of make-believe play to practice her new cognitive and motor skills.

You'll find her pouring invisible water and hammering invisible nails. Instead of just turning the wheel on her crib gym, she'll now use it to "drive." When she plays with her plastic containers alongside you in the kitchen, she'll be "cooking."

This shift into fantasy play is cute to watch, but it's also crucial for your baby's cognitive development. It helps her figure out how she can apply her newly discovered skills to real-life problems and experiences.

As she gets older fantasy also gives your baby a way to make sense out of the world around her. In make-believe she can be any age, male or female, rich or poor. She can be the mailman who comes every morning, the next-door neighbor or the household cat.

Through this play she discovers who *she* is and how she relates to the people, animals and objects around her. This process is critical for her developing self-esteem, and it also makes her much more sensitive to other people.

Watching your baby carefully as she engages in fantasy play may give you a little more insight into her real-life thoughts and feelings. You'll find clues to what interests her, and you may learn about some of the things that are troubling her. Many thoughts that she cannot express directly will come tumbling out in her fantasy play. It's a valuable release for your baby and a fascinating opportunity for you.

D I S C O V E R Y   P L A Y

Fantasy

One way to encourage fantasy play is to provide your child with the kind of props that suggest "pretend" activities. Set aside a low shelf in the kitchen for your baby's own "cooking utensils." Keep a miniature broom or vacuum cleaner alongside your cleaning equipment (but far away from dangerous chemical cleaning agents, please!). Provide her with a child's tool bench, typewriter, musical instruments or other toys that are likely to spark make-believe activities.

Be forewarned that your baby's fantasy activities may stretch your tolerance. A toddler's "cooking" project can get very messy, and you're not likely to laugh when your little garden helper "weeds out" your favorite tulips. Try to be patient and understanding. Supervise these make-believe sessions to prevent out-and-out calamity, but otherwise give your child as much free rein as possible. By encouraging fantasy play you'll bring out the best of your child's imagination and creativity.

· XII ·

Feeling: Your Baby's Social and Emotional Development

As you watch your newborn during her first weeks of life, you are bound to wonder what she's thinking, how she's feeling and what you can do to make her happy.

Watch her closely and you'll soon learn to read her signals of overall contentment and discomfort. But much of the mystery remains even after you've discovered these general signs. Why does she fuss or smile for no apparent reason? Why does she suddenly, between five and seven months, balk at the sight of her grandmother or next-door neighbor?

What is she thinking as she stares at you or babbles incoherently for minutes on end? No one can tell you for sure what's on her mind, but the latest research discoveries may help you find some general answers to these questions.

Babies as young as three months express feelings of contentment, anger, frustration and distress. Each child balances these emotions differently, depending on her own unique temperament. Some babies are active, some calm. Some tend to be fearful and cautious, others curious and outgoing. Some are slow to respond while others are extremely spontaneous.

These characteristics affect the way babies react to people, the ease with which they adjust to feeding and sleeping schedules, and their level of general fussiness—all the issues that concern parents most. Ordinarily, unless parents specifically force a change in the child's temperament, she will retain these basic personality traits throughout her life.

Child development experts believe babies need to establish a stronger frame of reference before they can feel more complex emotions like shyness, sadness, disgust, anxiety and guilt, which usually don't emerge until the second six months. This frame of reference consists of the love, comfort, security and care your baby receives in her early months. She depends on you to provide this base.

As she starts to recognize familiar people, places and toys, and develops her own routine, your baby begins to associate these things with her own happiness. That's when her emotions start coming out in force. For example, once she recognizes who you are, her face will light up in delight every time you enter the room. She'll be excited by experiences that vary slightly from her routine, and frightened by things that are too new and different from what she considers normal.

As your baby's memory develops, she begins to understand the principle of cause and effect and how it relates to her. With this discovery, her emotions become increasingly complex. Before this time she would rarely get upset if you took a toy away from her. By the age of eight months the same trick will make her furious, because now she is able to connect your action with her loss, and she will direct her anger at you.

Before the end of the first year your baby will be making predictions about the way the world works, and she'll be most content when it works exactly as she expects it to. If you show her a mechanical toy that goes off and on every four seconds, she'll take it in stride. If the same toy starts to operate erratically and unpredictably, she may become disturbed or alarmed.

But surprises like this are important for your baby. According to Harvard psychologist Jerome Kagan, it's the unexpected that keeps a child learning: "The nursery with a ten-unit mobile is not better than one with a six-unit mobile, but alternating from one to the other every five days might produce a more alert infant."

In the second year many new emotions start to emerge as the toddler explores and tests the world around her. She becomes upset when she encounters a task that's too difficult. She feels guilty when she does something she shouldn't.

She starts to develop empathy and will worry if she thinks you are hurt or even if you accidentally break a cup, because she can now imagine how it feels to be injured (in her mind the cup, like a person, can feel pain when broken). And she smiles with real pleasure when she does a job well because she has learned to value success over failure.

Through this entire process you play a crucial role in supporting, guiding and teaching her to cope with these new emotions. She depends on you to help her learn how to regulate these strange feelings and bring them to a healthy balance.

THE PARENT-CHILD CONNECTION

Your relationship with your baby begins in the very first moments after her birth. This period of bonding is important to you both. She is wide awake, alert and quietly receptive to you and everything around her. As you hold her and your eyes meet, she'll naturally cuddle toward you. Your touch, smell, voice and image all form the basis of the attachment she will develop for you in this first year.

What is attachment? It's the connection between two people who are attuned to each other's needs, wants, feelings and presence. Attachment provides the emotional foundation for your baby's personality. The more securely she becomes attached to you, the more secure she will be in the future. Attachment builds slowly and steadily as you get to know each other. The way you play together, the sounds and gestures you make to each other, the way you look at and touch each other all contribute to these feelings of connectedness.

A great deal of research has been done to find out what is required for a healthy attachment between parents and children. It's easy to say that parents should love their children without smothering them and provide security while encouraging independence, but any parent knows

it's not that simple. You're human, and you're bound to overreact from time to time out of frustration, anger or concern.

Then there are times when you just can't be with your child as much as you'd like. Does that mean your baby will grow up with a warped self-image? Probably not, as long as you maintain a reasonable balance. But what is that reasonable balance?

For many years this question was clouded by what seemed to be an international panic over "spoiling the child." Remember those wonderful not-distant-enough sayings: "Spare the rod and spoil the child," "Children should be seen and not heard," "Give 'em an inch and they'll take a mile"? Those ideas dictated the way many children were raised in this country before 1940.

For more than twenty years the country's leading pediatricians instructed mothers *never* to pick up their babies between feedings, no matter how much they cried. The idea was that mothers who paid attention to their babies' signals would encourage the babies to be more demanding and increase the amount they cried.

A landmark study by Johns Hopkins researchers Silvia Bell and Mary Ainsworth overturned this idea. The team observed twenty-six mothers and infants from birth through the first year. They watched how quickly mothers responded to their babies' cries and what kind of responses soothed babies best. They found that the sooner a mother responded to her baby, the more quickly the baby would quiet down. The most effective way to soothe a crying baby, they learned, is to pick her up and hold her. If that doesn't work, feeding her may.

The team also found that when mothers responded promptly and *consistently* to their babies' cries, the babies gradually stopped crying and fussing and became increasingly independent over the course of the first year. When mothers routinely ignored their babies' cries or waited a long time before responding, the babies became classic "spoiled brats"—crying, fussing, clinging and refusing to move out on their own.

According to Dr. Ainsworth, most babies older than a few months only call for their mothers when they need something specific, like food, or when they feel their relationship with the mother is endangered. Children who feel a normal, healthy attachment to their mothers typically go through a stage, which we'll talk about later in this chapter, when they cry each time their mothers leave them in a strange room or with a stranger.

This phase usually occurs around the end of the first year, when babies feel threatened by separation from their mothers. But a baby whose mother *consistently* has ignored her from birth feels that the relationship is threatened *all the time,* and cries whether or not her mother is nearby.

In most families the baby's most important relationship is with her mother. This is not necessarily because she is the one who takes care of the infant or has some special biological bond. It is probably because in most families the mother is the person who pays the most attention and spends the most time playing and talking with the child.

With today's fathers playing an increasingly important role in childrearing, researchers are just beginning to study the attachments of babies whose fathers stay home and care for them. Predictions are that equally strong attachments will develop between these fathers and their babies as most babies have with their mothers, assuming that the fathers are equally playful, loving and attentive with their children.

This is not to say that the typical father is a stranger to his child, or that the key attachment in a baby's life has to be a parent at all. Despite the fact that the average father in this country spends only fifteen to nineteen minutes a day playing with his baby, most children develop strong attachments to father and mother around the same time— eight months.

Babies this age also demonstrate strong attachments to siblings and familiar grandparents and baby-sitters. If the person who normally cares for the baby does not establish an emotional connection with her, the baby may turn to these other friends and family members for positive attachment. In cases of parental abuse or neglect, these other connections can be a true lifesaver for the child.

When no one is available to provide that emotional anchor, children may be retarded in a number of areas. In an orphanage in Iran, where babies were given minimal human contact and sensory stimulation, researchers found that only 14 percent of the children were able to crawl by one year, and only 15 percent could talk by the age of four.

Closer to home, studies show that babies of chronically depressed mothers act depressed themselves. They tend to be very passive and detached, mirroring their mothers' behavior.

Babies who have a healthy attachment to their mothers can't stand to see their mothers depressed. If the mothers intentionally (for the purpose of a study) begin speaking in a monotonous tone, moving listlessly, minimizing facial expression and contact with their infants, the babies become visibly upset.

These studies show that the critical issue is not whether you stay home with your baby every day, but how you share the time when you are together. If you're not "connecting" with your child, then both of you are missing a crucial element in your relationship. It's the old "quantity vs. quality" issue. Both are essential to your baby's health and happiness.

We want to stress that this process is not always smooth and pleasant, nor should it be. Your baby is bound to have cranky periods and so are you. You will have to learn to deal with each other's bad moods as well as the good. But remember that your responses largely determine the quality of attachment between you and your baby. She depends on you to show her that she's as important in your life as you are in hers.

STRANGER ANXIETY

A newborn baby views everyone as an ally, but as early as fourteen weeks after birth, she starts to separate the people in her universe into friends and strangers. She'll smile at her friends and look them squarely in the eye, but simply stare at strangers. By four or five months she will stop playing and may freeze up in fear when a strange adult comes too close. This is the beginning of what psychologists call "stranger anxiety." It's the first of many fears that emerge as your baby discovers she is a separate, vulnerable human being.

About half of all babies experience stranger anxiety. Whether your baby will go through this phase depends largely on her own personality. If she's inquisitive and enthusiastic about new experiences in general, she may well be immune to this fear. If she's extremely cautious and hesitant about trying new things, she probably will be just as reluctant to deal with strange people.

If your baby does experience stranger anxiety, she'll probably begin to show clear signs of it around six or seven months, the same time when many other complex emotions become apparent. Even people who are somewhat familiar, like relatives and neighbors, are suddenly off limits. If they try to pick her up she may scream, whimper, or simply stiffen and look away. This pattern may continue into her second year. As frustrating as this may be for all of you, don't push her to be friendly. She'll come around in time.

Here are some suggestions that will help put your baby at ease when you are with outsiders:

· The closer your baby is to you physically, the less upset she will be when someone new approaches her. Stay with her when she first meets a new person. Never give her immediately to someone else to hold or leave the room before she's relaxed.
· The more familiar the setting, the easier it will be for her to accept an unfamiliar person. If you have a choice between taking her to a friend's house or entertaining at home, stay home.
· Your responses to the stranger may also affect her. If you are relaxed and talk cheerfully to your baby about this new person, you may be able to put her at ease. (Some studies indicate that this strategy is more successful with calm, low-key babies than with more active, high-strung infants.)
· The more exposure your child has had to a variety of people, beginning early in infancy, the more comfortable she will be in new encounters. If your baby has a regular baby-sitter or is part of a play group or day-care program several times a week, she'll probably be more tolerant of strangers than if she is home with you alone every day.
· Babies are rarely afraid of strangers who are children—even children as old as twelve or thirteen. No one knows exactly why babies are more relaxed with children, but it's not just a matter of size because they are just as afraid of dwarfs as they are of

other adults. If there are other small children around, you may find that your baby is less fearful of strangers than if she's in a room full of adults.

If nothing seems to work and you need to leave your baby with someone on a regular basis, the following "program" may help her get acquainted with a minimum of trauma. It will probably take you about two weeks to reach Step 7.

Step 1   Place the child on your lap with a familiar toy in a familiar room and allow the new person to come in. Don't let the stranger talk to your baby or even make eye contact.

Step 2   Keeping your baby on your lap, allow the stranger to come closer, still without making eye contact or touching the child.

Step 3   Allow the stranger to make some eye contact with a broad smile and "hello," but no touching.

Step 4   Allow the stranger to talk to your child at length. If the baby fusses, have the stranger break eye contact, but remain in the room.

Step 5   Put the infant down at your feet and let the stranger get down on the floor near her with a toy between them. Stay close to the baby as she and the stranger play together.

Step 6   Gradually increase your distance while the stranger plays with your baby. When the child looks for you, avoid eye contact.

Step 7   Leave the room while the two of them are playing together. Once you can do this without your baby protesting, you're home free.

SEPARATION ANXIETY

In the first months of her life your baby is barely aware of any difference between herself and you. Gradually, as she begins to explore on her own and discover her own unique abilities, she realizes that she is a separate human being. But this realization comes before she fully understands the nature of your relationship. When you leave the room she is not at all sure you're going to come back. She doesn't even know whether you still exist. She gets frightened and protests every time you leave her. This is the beginning of separation anxiety.

This fear usually begins to emerge around the age of eight or nine months. Most babies will either kick, cry and try to follow their mothers or they'll become silent and morose at the first sign their mothers are leaving. After a long separation some infants will "punish" their mothers by ignoring them or pretending not to recognize them, all the while clinging to them for dear life.

Protesting when you leave is not the only way your baby may show attachment at this stage. She may cling to you or follow you from room to room. She may become especially clutchy outside the home, or when you are acting different than usual. Though she may be lured away from you briefly by an interesting toy, she will come back frequently to "touch base" and reassure herself that you are still there.

Only after she learns that you always reappear after a separation can she start to relax her grip on you. Try to act in a way that builds this trust. Never threaten—even in jest—to leave her behind. Instead, remind your baby that you will be back and constantly reassure her that she'll be fine while you are away.

While separation anxiety usually focuses most strongly on the mother, many infants show the same clutchiness for their fathers, siblings, grandparents or regular baby-sitters. Twins often become fearful and upset when separated from each other, the way other babies react when their mothers leave them. As a baby gets older and establishes close relationships with several different people, she may get upset whenever any of them leave her.

Most babies get over separation anxiety by the end of their second year. Exactly when your baby will pass through this phase—or whether she will demonstrate it at all—depends in part on her unique personality. Some children seem to be naturally vulnerable to fear, likely to cry at the slightest provocation and reluctant to venture forth on their own. These children have the hardest time letting their mothers out of their sight. Other, more easygoing babies tend to be more accepting of their mothers' departures and get past separation anxiety at an earlier age.

Children whose parents are extremely protective are more likely to panic when they're left behind. In essence, these babies have been taught that they can't survive without their parents, so they behave accordingly. These children do not necessarily love their mothers any more than the self-reliant babies, but they've been taught to have different expectations, and they've learned a different way to cope with their fear.

GROWING UP SOCIAL

Your relationship with your baby is her first and most important social experience, but she needs others even in these early months. Seeing other people, especially other children her age, helps her establish a sense of herself within a broader social world than your immediate family. These contacts are her first taste of friendship and companionship. They help her develop the skills and confidence she'll need to make friends of her own in the years to come.

Arrange for your baby to meet other children her age starting early in the first year. As she gets older, keep broadening her social network so she gets used to meeting new people and has a chance to choose special friends for herself. Day-care programs and play groups naturally provide your child with the right kind of social stimulation. So do mother-infant activity programs such as those offered by the YMCA. But you don't need to enroll in a formal program or class to provide this benefit to your baby. Take her often to the park or to the homes of friends who have children. This also gives you a valuable opportunity to compare notes with other parents.

When you bring children together initially, let them get to know each other without introducing toys. Infants as young as six months will usually gravitate toward each other and play together spontaneously if there are no distractions present. If you introduce a toy, the babies may be more interested in the toy than in each other. Once the children get to know each other and have established a solid rapport, you can try introducing toys to let them experiment with sharing and cooperating, but don't expect this process to be smooth sailing for some time. It often takes years for children to learn how to share their possessions and work together on play projects. Your best strategy is to stand back as much as possible. Tell your child that it's important to share and demonstrate that message through your own actions, but don't intervene in your child's social struggles unless one child is actually in danger of hurting the other.

STRANGE SITUATIONS

By the end of her first year your child will be keenly aware of everything that's happening around her. Some of these experiences, which she used to take in stride, will suddenly begin to frighten her at this time. She may be afraid of water, heights, loud noises or the dark. These fears show that she's learning the concept of danger.

On the positive side, these new anxieties may protect

her from some situations that really are dangerous. But they're no fun for her, and they may limit her exploration too much. Fortunately, you can help her regulate some of these fears and prevent her from being immobilized by them.

One of the ways your baby learns to react to new situations is by watching you. Researchers have found that twelve-month-olds who are confronted with a strange object will check their mothers' reaction before registering one of their own. If the mother's facial expression is neutral or frightened, the baby will immediately run toward her and away from the object. If the mother smiles, the baby will stay where she is and play with the toy, even if she's far from her mother.

Your voice, facial expressions and body movements all convey your emotions. If you act fearful, your baby will adopt that anxiety herself. If you smile and talk to her naturally, she'll relax, figuring everything must be okay. By staying with your baby, protecting her as you encourage her to strike out on her own, you'll help ease her past the worst of her fears. Soon nothing will hold her back.

WHAT'S BEST FOR YOUR BABY

When it comes to raising your child, no one can tell you for sure what's "best" or what's "right" beyond totally loving and accepting her. But a study of children by the Harvard Pre-School Project in the 1960s revealed some successful strategies. Four hundred preschoolers were divided into three groups according to their intellectual and emotional qualities. The "A" group was considered highly well-rounded and generally "excellent." The "B" group was considered average, and the "C" group children had difficulty coping with everyday life and learning. The researchers observed the parenting techniques used by mothers of children in each group. (They assumed that the mothers had the most important input in terms of parenting.) They discovered the following common denominators among the mothers of "A" group children:

· The mothers generally had a positive outlook on life.
· They were energetic, patient and tolerant of their children.
· They did not prevent their children from taking minor risks in play.
· They did not devote all their time to their children (many had part-time jobs).
· They "designed" interesting games and play environments full of stimulating objects and learning challenges.

The "C" group mothers also shared some common characteristics:

· They either spent very little or all their time with their children.
· They had relatively little physical contact with their children.
· They resented the fact that as their children grew up they explored more and tended to "get into" everything.

The critical difference between these groups is the understanding between parent and child. The "A" group mothers made the effort to understand and look at the world from their *children's* perspective. The "C" group mothers, for whatever reasons, couldn't demonstrate this understanding.

Most parents have an uncanny understanding of their children's thoughts and emotions. If they trust these perceptions and act accordingly, everyone does just fine. The trouble sets in when parents let doubt overstep confidence and try to conform to some idealized vision of how things "should be."

The easiest way to prevent unwarranted doubts and fears is, quite simply, to watch your baby closely. See what she looks at. Note the things that make her smile. Listen to her responses as you cuddle or sing to her. Notice when she moves around and when she prefers to lie quietly. Just as she lets you know when she's tired, wet and hungry, she also possesses a full repertoire of signals for her other needs and desires. It's easy to learn these signals if you're willing to tune in.

Tuning in also means respecting your baby's ups and downs. Know when to give her a rest. Just think how annoyed you are when people break into your daydreams or disrupt your train of thought. Your baby feels exactly the same way. If a baby is constantly pushed too hard when she doesn't want to be pushed, she may conclude that nothing she does makes a difference. This can have disastrous effects on her self-image and relationships with people around her.

Infant researchers, whose work demands that they tune in to babies, have identified several basic signals that indicate when a baby is attentive and when she's disinterested or overstimulated. Even the youngest infant can tell you when she's had enough. At first she'll look away. Then she may become glassy-eyed or look right through you. She may move her body to physically turn away or simply go limp. Finally, if all else fails, she may wail for escape. By getting to know and respect your baby's early warning signals you can spare both of you a lot of needless discomfort.

It's just as simple to tell when your baby is ready for play. She'll look you straight in the eye and "talk" to you. The talk may only be a syllable or two, or it may be a prolonged cooing, but you'll know from the tone and intensity whether she's in a good mood or bad. After a while you'll know what sounds, movements and activities make her happiest. You'll be able to pinpoint her favorite books, pictures, people, records and toys. During restless moments you can call on these special "friends" to calm her down.

These are the discoveries that will make you a better parent. If, in addition, you respect and have fun with your baby, if you give her the freedom and encouragement to discover the world around her and provide a home life that is warm and supportive, you can be sure you are creating the foundation for a lifetime of mutual trust, love and learning.

· XIII ·

Birth to
Four Months

Your baby will go through more changes in her first four months than at any other time in her life. Each day you'll see that she has acquired a new skill, grown a little, changed in appearance and become more alert to her surroundings. Several key developments in the first three months will transform your baby from a totally dependent newborn to a responsive, loving human being. These hallmarks of the first weeks of life include the following:

Smiling—Your baby will make smiling movements with her mouth from birth, but these do not develop into heartfelt, intentional smiles until the end of the first month or so. When the true social smile arrives, you'll know it because your baby's whole body becomes a part of it. Her eyes wrinkle, her body wiggles, and there is no doubt that this is an expression of feeling.

Visual Tracking—By the end of the second month your

baby's vision will be coordinated enough that she can follow a slowly moving object horizontally and vertically. Soon afterward, she'll be able to track circular movement. As soon as she achieves this skill, she'll far prefer moving objects to stationary ones and will spend long periods of time watching the motion of her mobile as it circles overhead.

Seeing Color—Throughout most of this phase your newborn is sensitive to varying degrees of brightness, but cannot detect the subtleties of hue. Toward the end of the third month, however, her eyes will have developed enough so that she can see the primary colors and some middle hues. As time goes by, she'll gradually learn to differentiate between colors that are close together.

Expanding Field of Vision—At birth your baby can only focus about eight to ten inches from her eyes (that's just about the distance between a mother's face and her baby's when she's nursing). Objects farther away are a blur. Her range of vision extends gradually during these first weeks and, by the end of this period, her eyesight should be almost as accurate as yours.

Localizing Sound—If her hearing is normal, your infant will now become quiet when stimulated with sound, especially the sound of your voice. She soon learns to place sounds as well and will follow a traveling noise with her eyes and body.

Grasping—In the first days after birth your baby's hands are usually clenched tight, but they begin to relax by the end of these first months. At the same time, her hands will become a source of fascination to her. She'll explore their shape and taste by sucking on them and staring at them. By the end of the third month she'll have discovered that hands can be used purposefully to hold and drop things. Although her grip may still be quite tentative at this point, she is beginning to practice the many ways that hands can be used as tools.

Arm and Leg Movements—Though her muscle control is still mostly reflex, your baby will begin to thrust her arms and legs and direct their movement. By the end of this period she may be able to roll over, hold her head up when sitting, and kick or swipe at toys in the crib.

The first few days and weeks can be very difficult for you, because your baby may give you very few visual cues and rewards. During the first month she probably will not smile back at you, and you may feel ignored and neglected. Rest assured, things will change. Continue to let her know that you are with her, interested in her and willing to play. By the second month she'll have discovered the magic of smiling and will delight you with her enthusiasm.

The purpose of Discovery Play at this stage is not to teach your child any specific skills, but rather to help the two of you get to know and trust each other. You'll learn to appreciate all the small conquests she makes each day, and she'll discover she can depend on you to share her delight in these accomplishments. These activities also will provide a safe and enjoyable way for you to help her practice her new abilities.

NEWBORN MOVEMENT PLAY

Your baby still lacks the strength and coordination to benefit from a formal physical exercise program. However, there are many physical activities you can do with your baby just for fun. The more you play with each other, the easier it will be to detect the small but important changes in her motor development that take place every day. If you look closely, you'll be amazed how much she is changing.

YOUR BABY'S REFLEXES

Your newborn's muscle activity during the first month of life is mainly governed by reflexes. If you familiarize yourself with these reflexes, you'll feel more comfortable about her sometimes odd behavior, and you'll learn to predict her reactions to her surroundings. You'll also be more likely to notice when these reflexes disappear or turn into intentional movements—both signs that your child is maturing.

D I S C O V E R Y   P L A Y

Reflexes

This chart will help you engage your child's reflexes and predict when they will disappear:

STIMULUS	RESPONSE	DISAPPEARS
(What You Do)	(What Infant Does)	(Approx.)
Make a loud sound or startle your infant	Both arms reach out in grasping fashion, head goes back, eyes open, may cry (Moro reflex)	three months

159

STIMULUS	RESPONSE	DISAPPEARS
Tap bridge of nose (gently)	Eyes close tightly	one–two months
Extend (straighten) arms at elbows, legs at knees	Arms and legs flex	three months
Pull baby to sit	Head falls back, shoulders tense, eyes open	one–two months
Put on stomach	Turns head to side, lifts head slightly, "swims" with arms and legs	two months
Place on back and twist head to side (gently)	Extends arm on the side her head is turned to, flexes other arm at shoulder (tonic neck reflex— fencer's position)	two months
Stroke top of foot or hand	Foot or hand withdraws	two–three months
Stroke palm or sole of foot	Hand or foot grasps	two–three months
Stroke outside of foot	Toes spread and big toe goes upward	one–two months

STIMULUS	RESPONSE	DISAPPEARS
Stroke cheek	Head turns toward the side that is stroked (rooting reflex)	four months
Place object over face	Mouth moves, head twists, arms flail to remove object	six months

BABY MASSAGE

Even the youngest newborn loves skin-to-skin contact. Holding and touching provide important cues to the new baby that she is protected, loved and cared for. Baby massage is an ideal way to provide this kind of stimulation. It will help her become more alert when she's waking up from a nap and calm her down when she's feeling irritable. Even a disruptive or noisy diaper change can sometimes be quieted by a gentle massage.

D I S C O V E R Y   P L A Y

Massage

The only equipment you need to perform baby massage is a quilt or blanket spread on the floor, some baby oil, soothing music and a naked baby. Try to set aside fifteen or twenty minutes so you can massage every part of your infant's body. Begin by laying her on her back. Using the baby oil to lubricate your hands, gently stroke her chest and shoulders in a circular motion. Then move your hands down each arm and massage each hand. Lift her legs one at a time and stroke from thigh to foot.

Massage each foot, including the toes, and gently rotate the foot from the ankle to relax and stretch it. Turn the baby over onto her abdomen and continue the massage across her back and shoulders, down to her buttocks and on down the backs of her legs to her feet. Feel the strength in her arms and legs as she goes through her normal swimming movements. She may seem tight and flexed at the elbows and knees, but this will gradually loosen up by the end of the first month.

BALANCE

When you rock your baby, you move the child in a way that causes stimulation of the vestibular (balance) mechanism in her inner ear. Babies respond to this motion and stimulation by becoming generally more alert and visually attentive to their surroundings. Steady rocking also calms most babies, so rocking your baby is a good way to get her in an attentive mood when you have something to show or tell her.

D I S C O V E R Y P L A Y

Balance

There are several different ways to provide vestibular stimulation, most of which you'll do naturally with your newborn. Among these:

- Rock your baby in your arms.
- Rock her in a rocking chair.
- Let her swing in an infant swing. (Make sure she's securely strapped in. Infants younger than one month are generally too small to use these seats.)
- Rock her in a cradle.
- Take her for a ride in a stroller or carriage.
- Lift her up from a sitting or lying position.
- Lay her stomach down atop a large inflated beach ball and gently roll her back and forth and side to side.
- Sit-ups and stand-ups:

By the end of the first month you can do "sit-ups" with your baby by holding her hands and pulling her up very gradually. Do this very slowly and smoothly at first, supporting her head with one hand until she has enough strength in her neck muscles to hold her head in line with her body. When she gets up all the way, reward her with a funny facial expression or

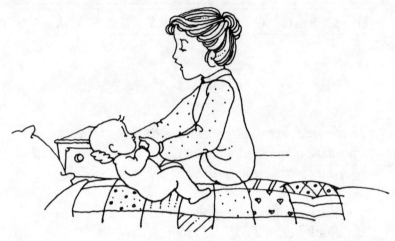

As you teach your two-month-old to sit up, be careful to support the back of her head.

sound. This activity strengthens her back, arms and neck muscles. By the end of the third month she may start to move toward you on her own as you begin to pull her up. She still can't remain seated by herself, however, so do not leave her side after she's completed her "sit-up."

By the end of the third month she will also love being pulled to a standing position and may take a few steps while being held. Many parents think this is the prelude to real walking, and they worry when walking does not quickly follow. In fact, this probably only reflects the remnant of a reflex and not true, early walking. At this point your baby is simply not strong enough in the necessary muscle groups to walk.

MUSCULAR CONTROL

By the second month your baby's movements are becoming much less reflexive and more controlled. When she sees something in front of her she can swipe at it, almost grasping for it. She loves to kick outward and often will become extremely animated, kicking and swiping at any object within reach—especially those that move in 're-sponse. Now is the time to provide crib toys that encourage this batting and kicking practice. The best ones use a rigid bar across the crib to suspend interchangeable ob-

Encourage your baby to reach and help develop her visual skills by suspending attractive toys above her in the crib. Make sure they are securely fastened and hanging no closer than ten inches from her face. Be sure to remove the suspension apparatus by five months or as soon as she can sit up alone.

jects that spin, swing, flash or make noises when the baby hits them. Adjust the objects so they hang toward the edges of the crib where your baby is more likely to look at them. Be sure she cannot pull the toys off or become entangled in any way.

If you'd rather make your own crib system, stretch very heavy elastic across the crib and *tie it well to both sides.* From this, hang simple objects that will attract your infant's attention: colored measuring spoons, rattles, wooden beads, plastic bangle bracelets, small stuffed animals. Make sure the objects cannot be pulled free. Hang them just low enough so the baby can reach them with her fingertips or toes, and don't use any objects small enough to be swallowed if they fall into the crib.

GRASPING

By the end of the first month your infant's grasp is more than just a reflex action. It is still a primitive, clawing motion rather than a fine finger grasp, but it serves her well as she begins to take a more active interest in objects around her. She'll delight in her own hand movements and her fledgling ability to bring objects to her mouth, where she can explore them orally as well as manually. Handling and mouthing are valuable sensory experiences for her and should not be discouraged. Your job is to provide her with safe objects to handle and mouth. They should be easy for her to grasp and manipulate, but at the same time large enough so she cannot swallow or choke on them.

Your baby is still too young for larger balls, blocks,

pyramids or finely detailed toys that require more complicated finger work. If you imitate your baby's grasp you
will realize the kinds of objects she can use. Look for solid
rods, rings and other shapes that fit easily into her palm.
Try balls with grooves in them, rings of different colors,
and rattles that have large rounded ends and a central rod
for her to grab onto.

D I S C O V E R Y   P L A Y

Grasping

*To help increase your infant's awareness of her hands,
seat her in your lap, take her hands and gently "clap"
them together in front of her and above her head. She
will like the stretching and the sight and feel of her
hands coming together. Slip brightly patterned bands
on her wrists or tie a bell (loosely) around one wrist
when she does this, and she'll like it even more.*

VISION

Even though your baby's field of vision is limited during
these first months, her eyes are among her most valuable
tools as she explores the world around her. The visual
stimulation you provide gives her an incentive to keep
looking and learning.

D I S C O V E R Y   P L A Y

Visual Games

• *Making Faces.* In her first weeks of life your face is the best toy of all for your baby. Infants even a few hours old will imitate many exaggerated facial expressions, such as an open mouth or an extended tongue, but just making eye contact is the most important part of this activity. You can often elicit this eye contact by gently rocking back and forth while holding your baby directly in front of you, face to face. Accompany these movements with soothing *oooh* and *aaah* sounds. Smile, grimace, laugh, stick out your tongue and use any other facial expression you can make. You may feel ridiculous at first, but that disappears quickly when your baby starts responding to you.

Remember that the optimum focusing distance between your face and your baby's is eight to ten inches during the first month of life. Month by month, you can gradually lengthen the viewing distance, watching her responses closely to see when she seems to lose her focus or interest. This will help you gauge how her vision is developing.

• *Tracking Practice.* Throughout this period your baby's range of vision will gradually expand,

and she will be able to follow objects through a wider arc of movement. You can facilitate development of tracking skills by providing moving targets for her to watch. At first, move them very, very slowly, always keeping them about eight to ten inches away from her face. Gradually increase the speed and range over the next few weeks. Here are some suggestions for tracking activities:

—Darken the room slightly, and move a flashlight side to side and up and down over your baby as she lies on her back. (Don't flash it directly in her eyes.)

—Lay her, stomach down, on the floor and roll a patterned ball back and forth in front of her.

—Hold her up in front of you and move her side to side and up and down. See how far you can move her before she loses track of your face.

• *Ribbon Fan.* Introduce your baby to the movement of wind and air with a ribbon fan. Make this fan by tying the ends of a dozen black and white ribbons (about ten inches long) to a plastic ring. Hang the ring outside near an open window or in front of an electric fan and position your baby's infant seat so she can watch the ribbons fly in the breeze. After a week or so, replace the plain ribbons with striped, checked or other patterned ribbons and see if the change increases her interest.

· *Mirror Play.* Toward the end of this period your baby will discover the magic of mirrors. Although she won't realize yet that the image in the mirror belongs to her, she will quickly learn that she can control the response of the mirror simply by moving. This is the ultimate in a responsive toy. For every move she makes, the mirror gives her an instant response. She will spend long minutes studying herself and experimenting with different movements of her face and body to see what the mirror will do in return.

Use only an unbreakable mirror, attached overhead or to the side of the crib where your baby looks most frequently. Try to position it just out of her reach, about eight inches away.

You may also want to secure a mirror alongside the changing table so she can entertain herself while you change her diapers.

• *Bubble Play.* Bubbles challenge your baby's developing vision. They offer movement for her to track as well as subtle colors and intriguing shapes to examine. In future months they'll also provide some fascinating lessons in object permanence, but for now they're simply fun to watch. You can blow bubbles with your baby seated in your lap or lying on her back next to you. Just make sure you don't blow the bubbles directly into her face or the soap will sting her eyes.

PATTERNS AND CONTRAST

Little babies love patterns, starting with simple checkerboards and bull's-eyes in the first month and gradually increasing in complexity as time goes on. Black-and-white figures and patterns provide the maximum contrast and will therefore be most interesting to your baby during her first few weeks. Begin introducing colored patterns of different brightness values by the end of the second month, but don't expect her to appreciate the full range of rainbow hues until her fourth month.

DISCOVERY PLAY

Patterns and Contrast

You can expose your infant to lots of different patterns in the course of her daily routine. Remember to vary them frequently; the more novel they are, the more interesting they'll be to her. Here are some simple suggestions:

1. Attach black-and-white checkerboards and bull's-eyes with tape to the side of your baby's crib or to the crib bumper. After a week or so change the patterns to more complicated arrangements and see if it affects her interest.

2. Play with lights, flashlights and shadows. You'll see her open her eyes widely when placed in the dark. This is a normal reflex.

3. Take large black-and-white photographs or cut out interesting shapes from magazines and let your baby see them. Show her a variety of different shapes and colors, and see if she seems to prefer some more than others.

4. Make up the crib with patterned sheets. It will be difficult to find these in black and white, but contrasting colors such as yellow and green or red and white will do quite well. Get several different sets so you can change them regularly.

5. Shop for stiff, high-contrast, patterned cloths that you can arrange within your baby's focal range. Take a square-foot piece, pinch it into a small peak and stand it on the floor or mattress next to her. The cloth will look like an object to your baby, but it has no hard edges and is safe to leave in the crib or play yard with her.

6. Make "plate faces." Using a white paper plate and a dark marker pen, draw a happy face on one side of the plate and a sad face on the other. Tie a ribbon to the top of the plate and hang it close to your baby. See if she notices the difference between the two faces as you slowly spin the plate around.

*7. The Variable Mobile. The most valuable gift
you can give your baby during this period is an
interesting mobile with interchangeable figures.
For the first couple of months your baby will be
content to stare at it, taking in the hundreds of
different shapes and images it creates as it turns
and shifts. By about the tenth week, however,
she'll be ready to take a more active role in playing with the mobile.*

*You can outfit your mobile with homemade shapes and figures,
using durable cardboard on which you've drawn high-contrast
patterns.*

The following tips will help you select and set up a mobile so your child gets the most benefit from it:

a. Look for mobiles that are either black and white or brightly colored. Tiny babies cannot see pastel shades well enough to appreciate them.

b. Place the mobile over one side of the crib or changing table, not over the center. Watch your baby to see if she has a favorite side. (Most babies tend to look to the right.) If she does, hang the mobile on the side where she looks most often, but change it periodically to see how she reacts.

c. Hang the mobile so the objects are from ten to thirteen inches away from the baby's eyes during the first two months. You may want to pull it back a bit in the third month as her vision develops and she becomes more physically active (and, therefore, potentially able to reach the mobile).

d. Gather a collection of alternative figures to hang on the mobile. Look for high-contrast images in bold patterns. Avoid miniatures with fine details that your baby won't be able to see clearly. Faces are ideal. So are geometric patterns and letters or numbers. *You may want to make your own figures out of high-contrast blocks, cutout shapes of paper or small toys.*

e. *Make subtle changes in the mobile every few days to challenge your baby's interest. Change the number of figures hanging from the arm. Switch one type of figure for another. Change just one or two figures at a time. Watch how your baby reacts to each of these changes. Recognition of these subtle changes is a good sign that her memory is developing.*

f. *Start giving her opportunities to manipulate the mobile when she's about ten weeks old. Tie one end of a soft ribbon to the middle of the arm of the mobile and the other end loosely to your baby's ankle or wrist. (Be sure the arm of the mobile is securely attached to the crib. Follow safety instructions on page 52.) Then stand back and watch as your baby begins to play. After a few minutes, change the ribbon to the other ankle or wrist and see how long it takes her to discover she must change her movements to get the mobile to respond. Let this game continue for up to half an hour if your baby remains engrossed in it. Take the ribbon off if she gets bored or if you must leave her alone. This*

*will probably remain one of your baby's
favorite games until she begins to crawl.*

HEARING DEVELOPMENT

The most important sound in your newborn's world is
your voice. She loves to hear you talk, sing, chatter and
laugh. You won't hear much from her at first except an
occasional grunt, coo or the obvious cry. As the first
month draws to a close, however, you will begin to hear
more and more responses.

By the second month, the first rudimentary sounds of
talking begin to appear. What had been only occasional
sounds of pleasure or crying are now punctuated by more
distinct sounds. The first noises come from the back of the
baby's throat and sound something like coughs or grunts.
These sounds, which are the first traces of vowels (*aaaaa,
eeeee, ooooooo*) are the beginning of a repertoire which
your baby will soon shape into an early form of communication.

D I S C O V E R Y   P L A Y

Song and Rhythm

• *Sound Searches. Challenge your baby to search
for the sources of sounds around her. Jingle a
bell in front of her to catch her attention, then*

sound the bell again to her side and see if she looks over to find it. In the first month she'll quiet, but not look over to exactly where the sound is. By the end of this period she'll turn quite consistently to the source of the sound and may even start to reach for it. Try moving the sound up, down and to both sides. You can also play this game with a rattle or other toy noisemaker. Just make sure the noise isn't so shrill or jarring that it startles your baby.

Tiny babies delight in rhythmic verse and songs. Whenever you run out of general conversation, entertain your baby by reciting or singing to her. Nursery rhymes, lullabies, college cheers and favorite ballads all make perfect source material. Limericks are ideal because they tend to be repetitive, rhythmic and full of easily differentiated sounds. Concentrate on songs or verse with simple, prolonged vowel sounds and consonants. "Baa, Baa, Black Sheep" is a good example of a song with sounds that appeal to babies.

Baa, baa, black sheep,
Have you any wool?
"Yes, marry, have I,
Three bags full;
One for my master,
And one for my dame,
And one for the little boy
Who lives in the lane."

You may want to collect recordings of children's songs with which you can sing along. Vary the tempo and volume of your selections to match the baby's mood, and move her arms and legs or dance her around the room in time with the music. If you play these songs regularly, your baby will soon start "singing" along by using her own repertoire of sounds and movements.

Introduce your baby to the sounds and songs of different parts of the world. Even if you don't speak another language, you can play recordings of music from other countries for your baby. Also, expose your baby to many different kinds of instruments with more exotic sounds, such as the sitar, harpsichord, music box and lute. This is the time to let your child know how wonderfully varied the world of sound can be.

- *Bells and Rattles.* Even at this early age you can give your newborn the chance to make music on her own. Attach small bells securely to a loose band and let her wear it on her wrists or ankles so her movements are rewarded with jingling. Some toy manufacturers now make infant bracelets with built-in rattles that accomplish the same purpose. Once your baby is able to grasp, consider getting her an infant xylophone or a small drum of her own.
- *Environmental Sounds.* Try to expose your baby to as many different environmental sounds as possible. Among the best sources of

sound stimulation are music, voices, common household sounds, passing trucks, singing, radios and stereos (without headphones). The last thing in the world you want to do is to insist that your infant's nursery be quiet day in and day out.

Another way to enrich your child's experiences with sound is to vary her environment. Take her with you as often as possible on errands, to the park, to the beach, on short hikes in the country. If you live in the city, try to find recordings that include the sounds of surf, birds and other animals. When you play such recordings, show your baby pictures that match the sounds.

- *Family Tapes. Make tape recordings of the different members of your family, individually and together. Also record your baby's own early babblings. Playing these tapes softly to your baby may be very soothing to her when she's alone in her crib.*
- *Rhythmic Noises. In the first months of life most babies are comforted by any rhythmic sounds that remind them of mother's heartbeat and the gentle whooshing noises of the womb. Several products that create these specific sensations are sold now, but you can create a similar effect by placing a ticking clock or metronome beside your infant's crib. You could even make a tape recording of your*

*washing machine to play as your baby lies in
her room.*

SMELL AND TOUCH

At birth your baby is even more sensitive to smell and
tactile sensations than you are. Within the first couple of
weeks she can distinguish between her mother's scent and
the scents of other people. She also knows—apparently
instinctively—which smells she likes best.

She is equally alert to different textures against her skin.
During the first three months your newborn's favorite sensation will be skin-to-skin contact, but she will be fascinated by the many other textures in her environment as
well.

D I S C O V E R Y P L A Y

Smell and Touch

- *Sniff Samples. Cautiously share the scent of
your perfumes or after-shave lotions with your
baby, using cotton swabs as samplers. The
newly developed "scratch'n'sniff" patches
offer an inexpensive and nontoxic way to provide her with a wide variety of pleasant smells.
(The only drawback is that most of these arti-*

181

ficial smells are not as pleasing as natural
scents.)
- *Texture Samples.* As your baby becomes more
inquisitive about touching, surround her with
lots of different textures to explore. Use a variety of fabrics such as velveteen, sheepskin,
satin, soft cotton and lambswool to line her
crib and cover her when she sleeps. Give her
lots of different textured objects to touch and
handle (be sure they're unbreakable and large
enough so they can't be swallowed). Some suggestions: bean bags, smooth plastic blocks and
balls, a glossy apple or bumpy orange, a swatch
of carpeting or rubber, a tiny wicker basket.
Watch how differently she responds to each
texture and see if she develops any favorites.
- *Stroking Sensations.* When you're dressing or
changing your baby, stroke her naked body to
give her different sensations. Use a soft water-
color brush, a feather, tufts of cotton, a mohair
or silk scarf. You can make a special "stroking
glove" by taking an old glove and taping fabrics or materials with different textures to each
finger. See how your baby's responses change
as you run each finger across her stomach or
arm.

SOCIAL DEVELOPMENT

These early months are the period when your baby comes
alive socially. This is when she learns what magic there is

in a smile, when she figures out that she's a person like you. Although it will be a few months yet before she fully comprehends the special nature of your relationship, she is becoming more familiar with you every day. Everything you do together enhances this familiarity, but there are a few activities you can do specifically to better understand your baby's perspective and she, yours.

DISCOVERY PLAY

Social Games

- *The Baby's-eye View. As often as possible, get down on the floor with your baby and see how the world appears to her. Notice how the furniture towers overhead, how far away the ceiling seems, how large the most commonplace objects in your household appear. Take this perspective into consideration when your baby has an unexpected reaction to new surroundings or events that happen around her.*

  For the same reason, bring your baby up to your level whenever you can so that she can see the world from an upright adult's view. Use a body carrier to hold her. This will let her watch the world go by from an upright position as you go about your daily routine.

VERBAL COMMUNICATION

Communication is one of the foundations of human social life, and your baby needs it just as much as you do. Your conversations with your baby not only lay essential groundwork for future language development, they also let her know you love her and respect her as a friend and loved one. This is why you should talk to your baby freely from the day she is born.

The sounds that your baby is practicing toward the end of this period are mainly the repetitive vowel sounds. Say them back to her, then mix up the vowels with some of the easier consonants (D, M, T, L). She won't be ready to make all of these sounds herself for another few months, but she'll watch and listen with great interest nevertheless. You both will feel as though you're having an active conversation.

D I S C O V E R Y   P L A Y

Language

- *Reading. It's never too early to begin reading to your child, even if she doesn't understand the specific meanings of the words. The purpose of this is to help her learn to associate the comfort and pleasure of the experience with the presence of books and printed words, not to teach her to read.*

In the beginning, pick out books with heavy cardboard or vinyl pages and very large print, with just a few words on a page. The illustrations also should be large and bold. (Save the delicately detailed picture books until your child is at least two.) Look for books with textures to them and run your baby's hand over the textures. Let her handle the books as much as she wishes. With luck, you may find that books become her favorite toys. The more she feels that books are "friends," the more eager she'll be to learn to read when the time comes.

- *Conversation.* Using plain simple language— not baby talk—tell her what you are doing whenever you are together. While bathing or changing her, name the parts of her body as you move them. As you walk down the street, tell her the names of the neighbors you pass. When you prepare dinner, talk about the different foods you're handling as you show them to her. It doesn't matter that she is too young to taste the foods or understand precisely what you are saying. Eventually all the things you tell her will fall into place. For the moment, the feeling of belonging is the primary benefit of this constant and close communication.

· XIV ·

Four to

Seven Months

This period marks the beginning of your baby's journey away from home base (that's you) and into the surrounding world. This is a transitional period when babies typically are torn between their attachment to familiar people and things and their intense curiosity about the world beyond.

Exploration comes naturally to your infant now as she starts to move about independently. She learns to roll over. Gradually, she starts to sit without support and, toward the end of the period, develops the skills she needs for creeping. This signals the beginning of full mobility, so clear the decks and adopt a positive attitude. The more freedom your baby has to move around, the more she will learn.

Independent locomotion is one of the greatest achievements of this developmental stage, but it's certainly not your baby's only coup. Among the others:

Babbling—Your infant has now discovered what fun it is to be verbal. She will converse with you for long periods at a stretch. She'll chatter, yell, shriek and even sing as she explores the full range of vocalization.

Reaching—The hand-eye connection becomes well established during this period, and your baby will reach eagerly for any attractive object or substance in sight. If she achieves her target, she'll happily grab it and steer it toward her mouth for further examination.

The Pincer Grasp—Her pincer grasp is firmly established by the end of this period. She loves to manipulate objects, transfer them from one hand to the other and stick her fingers into everything. Her hands and feet are her favorite play tools, and she will stare at them in endless fascination as she works her fingers and toes. Playtime and mealtimes give her wonderful opportunities to perfect these newfound skills and incorporate them into her ever-expanding repertoire.

Social Responses—During this period your baby learns to recognize many of the people who are around her every day, and she may become disturbed by the presence of strangers. She is beginning to understand that she is a unique individual and will start to show pride and pleasure in her own accomplishments. As a result, Discovery Play becomes a much more social activity than it was previously.

Memory—By the end of this period the saying "out of sight, out of mind" no longer applies because your baby's memory is developing. She now remembers objects after they leave her sight and will search for them and reach after them. If you leave her alone now, she wonders where you've gone and may call out to you if you are in another part of the house.

Discovery Play during these months is much more lively than in the first weeks of life. Your baby becomes an active participant who welcomes any opportunities you give her to practice her developing skills and engage you in "conversation."

MUSCULAR CONTROL

By this point most of your infant's early reflexes have disappeared, and she has much more direct control over her muscular movements. Watch the way she uses her hands now. Instead of grasping with a pawlike motion, she moves each finger independently to touch, manipulate and explore objects. Although it may be some time before she can pick up small objects with her thumb and forefinger, she has perfected the skills of reaching, grasping, holding on, twisting and dropping larger objects, both with one hand and two.

As she lies on her stomach, she'll make eager swimming movements with her arms and legs and arch her back in a way that makes her look like a small airplane getting ready to take off. As her arms become stronger, she will push her upper body off the ground in order to look or move around. Early in this period she will probably discover that she can push herself all the way and roll over onto her back. By the end of this period she'll also figure out how to reverse the maneuver. (Some babies roll from back to front first; this, too, is normal.)

As her back and neck muscles get stronger, she becomes increasingly adept at sitting by herself. By the end of this phase she may be strong enough to sit without support for half an hour or longer. She may even be able to push herself up into a sitting position without assistance.

Down on the floor, your baby probably will begin creeping around at this time. Using her arms to support her upper body and steer and her legs to push herself forward, she can move backward and forward at a surprising speed.

Although not all babies creep before they crawl—and some never creep at all—the usual sequence of locomotion is creeping, then crawling, then standing and walking by the start of the second year. The activities you do together will not necessarily speed up this process, but they will help your little one develop the confidence and strength she needs each step of the way.

D I S C O V E R Y P L A Y

Motor Skills

- *Rolling Practice. Help your baby get the feel of rolling over by placing her on a slight incline (a sloping pillow will do quite nicely). Rock her back and forth, then gently let her roll over. You can also lay her on a quilt or blanket, then lift up one side of it so she rolls from her stomach to her back. Talk to her quietly as you play and, if she fusses at this new sensation, stop and wait until she is ready for it.*

- *Pushing Off.* You can help your baby discover the thrill of crawling by placing her stomach down on a flat, clean surface and holding your palms against the soles of her feet. Don't push her or force her. Just hold your hands steady, and she'll push off and inch forward. Babies as young as three months can move several feet this way.
- *Jumpers.* Long before your child can walk she'll delight in jumping with the help of a hanging "jumper." These seats hang from the overhead frame in a doorway. They have elasticized straps so the baby gets an exaggerated bounce each time she pushes off with her feet. A jumper gives your baby the satisfaction of being upright and controlling her own movement while keeping her safe (as long as you use it in a wide doorway where she won't bump her head if she swings to the side).

  It may take her a few sessions to learn how to control her jumps, but once she has the hang of this, it will become her favorite activity. You can join in her fun by playing a jumping version of musical chairs. Jump with her a few times, then stop suddenly. Wait until she stops too, then start again. She'll soon catch on to this imitation game, and you can let her be the leader.
- *Target Socks and Wrist Bands.* Playing with hands and feet is an important activity in the early weeks of this period. Most babies are naturally attracted to their fingers and toes, but

you can heighten the fun of discovery by placing brightly colored socks on your baby's feet or patterned bands on her wrists. You can make these bands by cutting the top off a sock or by cutting the fingers off a mitten or glove (you want her fingers exposed so she can mouth them and explore with them). As an added attraction, attach bells or brightly colored tufts of yarn to the socks or wristbands.

• *Floor Play.* As your baby sits on the rug or the floor, surround her with large colored objects that she can reach for. See how curious she is by placing them just out of reach.

At first she might lose interest, but after awhile she will begin to reach actively toward her target. Don't place the toys so far away that she becomes frustrated. If she fusses, move them within her reach. As she begins to creep, lengthen the distance between her and these objects. This makes the game more interesting and helps her learn how to grab and creep at the same time. By the seventh month there will be no holding her back.

• *Creeping and Crawling.* As your baby gets more proficient at creeping and then begins to crawl, give her some obstacles (a pillow, cushion or folded quilt will do) to crawl over, on and around. Place a toy she likes on the other side of these obstacles. She may have difficulty finding it at first, but as she gets more practice at this game, she will soon catch on.

• *Mealtime Play.* Once your baby can sit up and

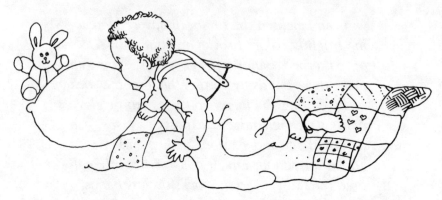

Help your baby develop her crawling skills by placing a toy on the other side of a soft obstacle.

starts to eat solid foods, mealtimes become perfect opportunities for her to practice fine motor skills. Though feeding time becomes increasingly chaotic as she begins to feed herself, the chaos is also part of learning. See what different-sized pieces she can pick up and how her pincer grasp is progressing. The following are ideal finger foods for babies at this stage:

Bagels (great for teething, too)
Spaghetti and pastas of various shapes
    (well-cooked)
Cooked carrots (sliced and quartered)
Small pieces of *peeled* apple

VISION

By four months your baby should be able to see in full color and with a full range of focus. She can see clearly objects all the way across the room. If you move a toy back and forth in a wide arc, she'll probably be able to follow it with little difficulty. Her improved vision makes her a much more active participant in play and adds to her pleasure as she takes in the people, places and objects around her. By providing her with plenty of stimulating things to watch and visual games to play (not television), you'll help improve her visual coordination and awareness.

D I S C O V E R Y   P L A Y

Discovery Play: Visual Games

- *Upside Down. At this age your baby will probably become fascinated with the way things look upside down. Here are a few activities to help her explore this new perspective:*
  —Stand with your back to her and bend down so that she sees your face upside down (through your legs).
  —Lay her on your knees and let her throw her head back to look at the room upside down (she'll do this spontaneously without any prompting from you).
  —Take a large beach ball and lay her, back down, on top of it. Holding her securely, gently roll her back and forth for a few seconds so she can watch the room moving upside down.
- *Roly-Poly Toys. These are the toys that spring*

back up when you knock them down to the side. Your baby will enjoy watching the rocking motion, especially if you use a toy with visible inside parts that move. She will also have a wonderful time reaching out and batting it.

- *Face Plates.* Your baby's favorite image remains the human face. During this period she decides what a proper face should look like and can tell that something is wrong when the eyes and mouth are out of place. Let her show you what she considers a proper face, using special "face plates." On one side draw a proper face and on the other side make a distorted face with the features in the wrong positions. Hold the plate up for your baby to see and flip it from one side to the other. Watch how your baby responds. Now leave it "wrong" side up. At some point most babies will turn the plate over to look at the "correct" face.

- *Tracing.* Equip your baby's nursery with large picture books, posters and fabrics printed with familiar images. During quiet times, use your finger to trace the borders of these pictures and watch to see if your baby follows your tracing. If she seems cooperative, take her fingers in yours as you make the tracing. Eventually, she'll be able to trace the pictures on her own. This practice helps build her observational skills and serves as a valuable prelude to writing and drawing later on.

HEARING

During this period your infant becomes increasingly attuned to the subtleties of sound. She can pick out familiar voices in a room full of people. She will recognize familiar tunes and may even hum or sing along with you. Experimenting with sound will give her hours of pleasure and enhance her sensitivity to the environment in the coming months. Bring out this natural interest by offering her a wide range of noisemaking options throughout the day.

D I S C O V E R Y   P L A Y

Language and Sounds

• *Instant Playback. During this period your baby will become a great chatterer. Her vocabulary consists of many distinct syllables, like ba, ma, ga and goo strung together in various combinations. Each few days she may experiment with a new sound, rolling it around in her mouth and testing it at different volumes and tones. Encourage this early talking by saying the sounds back to her. Enunciate clearly so she sees how your mouth moves to form her "word." Then tell her some real words that are made from similar sounds. For example, if her sound-of-the-week is ba, introduce her to the words baby, bar, babble, ball, belly, bounce, etc. Show her the objects or actions as you say these words.*

- *Read Along.* At this age your child is reaching out to touch anything she sees, and the books you read to her are no exception. Arm yourself with a good supply of cloth or stiff-paged books that will stand up to this mauling and let her go at them during storytime. Let her turn the pages and "feel" the pictures as you read to her. Select books with print as large as possible and follow along with your finger from word to word. The idea is to introduce her to all aspects of the reading process so she starts to connect the squiggles on the page with the words she hears.
- *Action Songs.* From this age on through toddlerhood your baby will adore songs that combine with body movement or dancing. "Hokey Pokey," "Ring Around the Rosey," "Pop Goes the Weasel" and "Eensy Weensy Spider" are all old favorites that work as well with babies today as they did in our parents' time. You can turn almost any familiar tune into an action song by adjusting the lyrics. Here's how Old MacDonald goes into action:

> Old MacDonald had a gym
> E-I-E-I-O
> And in that gym he had some knees
>   (or legs, arms, etc.)
> E-I-E-I-O
> With a bend, bend here
>   (or stretch, up, down, lift, etc.)
> A bend, bend there

Here a bend, there a bend
Everywhere a bend, bend
Old MacDonald had a gym
E-I-E-I-O.

- *Rattles.* Now is the time when your baby will have the most fun with rattles. She can pick them up, wave them about and drop them, all of which produce different, interesting sounds. Provide her with several different kinds of rattles at the same time so she can choose her own. Before long, she'll have one in each hand. Sing or count along as she creates her own unique rhythms. Make sure the rattle size is large enough to prevent the possibility of choking.
- *Animal Sounds.* By now your baby can tell the difference between your normal speaking voice and your "funny sounds." Try making animal sounds—mooing, chirping, barking, meowing, etc. See which ones she likes best. She'll probably let you know by her bursts of laughter.
- *Bangers.* Let your infant make her own sounds with household noisemakers such as aluminum pie tins, spoons and *plastic* soda bottles (empty and clean). Sit her on your lap at the table and show her how to bang her hands on the surface. This activity helps her practice different ways of grasping and also gives her the satisfaction of creating several kinds of noises.
- *Sound Jars.* Make sound jars out of *plastic* bottles (with caps) that you fill to different levels

with water, sand or other fillers. Using a wooden or plastic spoon, show your baby how each bottle produces a different sound when struck. As she fine-tunes her grip and reach, let her try hitting the bottles to make her own music.

SMELL, TASTE AND TOUCH

Your baby is becoming increasingly aware of the different qualities of objects and is especially keen on touching, tasting and smelling different things. This kind of sensory exploration adds an important dimension to her awareness of the world. Obviously, you must protect her from contact with objects and substances that could injure her, but you don't want to overprotect her. The best way to accomplish this is by providing her with objects that are safe to taste and touch and ridding the immediate environment of everything else.

D I S C O V E R Y   P L A Y

Smell, Taste and Touch

- *Warm and Cold. This is a good time to help your baby learn to distinguish differences in temperature. Offer her samples of water, milk, bread and other basic foods in both warm and cold form. Explain that one is warm and the other cold. See which she prefers.*

- *Scent Books.* Use scented stickers to make a set of "scent books" out of old booklets or a small notebook. Put a different scent on each page and let your baby sniff each page as you "read" the books together.
- *Grabbers.* At this age your baby will grab onto just about anything that comes her way, so why not provide her with some interesting textures and shapes to feel as she grabs? Collect an assortment of paper tubes (the center of a toilet paper roll is ideal). Cover each one with scraps of textured fabric or yarn, using a nontoxic glue. These textures give your child an unexpected reward as she practices her new grasping skills.
- *Texture Grab Bag.* Collect an assortment of safe materials with different textures. Samples of carpeting, satin, rubber, paper, foam rubber and smooth plastic all provide strong touch sensations. Make sure the samples are small enough for your baby to hold, but large enough so she can't swallow them. Place your collection in a cloth bag and let her pull one sample out at a time. Describe the sensation she's feeling (rough, smooth, rubbery, soft) as she explores the texture.

SOCIAL DEVELOPMENT

This is an especially important social period in your child's life because she is just beginning to understand the difference between herself and other people around her. She also loves to show off and will be intensely receptive to the responses of other people. With the least amount of encouragement, she'll entertain you for hours.

Most babies become increasingly sensitive to the presence of strangers during these months. Your baby is likely to be upset by strangers who "come on" very fast and strong, especially when you are not around to reassure her that all is well. Children who are cared for solely by their mothers all day long are most prone to this stranger anxiety. If your child has been cared for routinely by both parents, a regular baby-sitter or attentive day-care workers, she probably will not have as much trouble with strangers.

Your baby's full range of emotions also becomes evident now. She laughs easily and loudly, but also may get very angry and sullen when things do not go her way. Toward the end of this period, her emotional swings may vary from moment to moment. As easily as she loses her temper, however, she can be distracted by a funny toy or a silly face and quickly guided back to a pleasant mood.

Having a sense of humor will help you through these changes and make them much more fun for both you and your baby. Here are some activities that can help you make the most of these sociable months.

D I S C O V E R Y   P L A Y

Social Games

- *Imitations. Your baby takes great delight in imitating gestures and facial expressions. This*

is a wonderful way for her to try out movements that she might not discover on her own.
Draw her into imitative play by exaggerating
and simplifying your own expressions and gestures. Hold each one long enough for her to
track and follow before you move on to the
next. Exaggerating the movements of your
mouth as you make sounds will show her how
to put her mouth into shapes that will help her
learn to speak later. No doubt you'll discover
your own favorite moves, but here are some
suggestions to get you started:

Facial Expressions—broad smile, pout, surprised open mouth, laughing, wrinkled nose,
furrowed brow
Verbal Expressions—all the vowels and consonants in combinations such as *wah, baa, dee,
pah, fah, pee*
Simple Hand Movements—pointing, waving
good-bye, patting, clapping, making a fist and
opening it, touching finger to nose
Head Movements—nodding, shaking "no"
(side to side)

• *Family Pictures.* Your "family" may consist of
just three people or it may include many close
neighbors, friends and relatives. Help your
baby sort out the strangers from her family by
surrounding her with pictures of the important
people in her life. Keep these photographs
near her crib, changing table, play area and
eating place. Tell her who each person is by

name and talk about the role that individual plays in her life. When the person is nearby, let her compare the photo with the real-life version and see if she makes the connection. The more exposure she has to an individual, the more comfortable she will feel with him or her.

• *Mirror Play.* One of the best ways for your baby to come to terms with her sense of "self vs. others" is to explore the many different images available to her in mirrors. By watching herself move in the mirror, she gradually learns that this image belongs to her and her alone.

Through the mirror she can experiment with a wide array of movements and emotional expressions. Equip her with her own unbreakable mirror (about four or five inches in diameter) and also expose her to full-length mirrors around the house.

The full-length mirrors will help her discover that she is separate from you. She'll be perplexed at first as you move in and out of the reflection with her. Eventually she'll realize that you and she are two separate people who can be together or apart. By the end of this period your baby probably will react to the mirror as a playmate—almost a twin—and show joy and fascination with it. The mirror becomes a way for her to demonstrate the degree of security she feels about herself.

COGNITIVE DEVELOPMENT

At this stage, your baby is fascinated by the way objects look and work. As her memory develops, she becomes increasingly aware that objects and people continue to exist even when they are out of sight. She learns to anticipate the actions of people and objects around her. She becomes familiar with the ways they respond to her actions. Although she still has a long way to go before she can talk, your infant is already processing the information she needs to label objects, people and concepts. This ability to recognize words and names will soon become evident to you by the different ways she responds when you talk to her.

Now is the time to start providing your baby with simple problem-solving tasks and memory challenges. Research shows that she will regard these intellectual challenges as play. But it's important to remember that she will get frustrated quickly if you give her tasks that are too far beyond her ability. Watch carefully to see how she is faring. Don't do everything for her, but if you sense she needs a little help to succeed, don't hesitate to give it to her.

D I S C O V E R Y   P L A Y

Cognition

- *Three Toys at a Time. Give your child one toy for each hand, then present her with a third.*

See what she does. Most likely she will try to handle all three at once (without much success). Eventually, she'll solve the problem by putting one toy down before reaching for the third. Give her a chance to figure this out for herself. If it gets too frustrating for her, try a gentle demonstration.

• *Hidden Objects.* Challenge your baby to figure out what happens to objects when they're covered or blocked from sight. To begin with, take a favorite toy and cover half of it with a cloth. Name the toy and encourage her to get it and play with it. She may not recognize the hidden toy at first, but eventually she'll learn to pull it out or remove the cloth.

Once she has mastered the half-hidden object, try concealing it completely. Once she learns to uncover fully hidden objects, impose a delay between the moment you hide the object and the moment you let her uncover it. The longer she has to wait, the harder it will be for her to remember what is beneath the cloth.

• *Bathing Play.* The bath is a great place for your baby to discover the properties of liquids and concepts such as "under," "inside" and "outside." Provide her with shaped bath toys and sponges, and containers of assorted shapes and sizes. Encourage her to pick them up, bat them, try to sink them. Although she has not perfected the concept of "under water" this can be stimulated by putting objects under

water and asking her to go after them. At first she will be confused, but as you help her, she'll get the idea and go for them herself.

- *Peekaboo.* This is great fun for both of you and is also a lesson in object permanence for your infant. At first, you'll be the active participant, hiding your face behind your hands, a blanket or some other barrier. By six or seven months, though, your baby will enjoy covering her own face and then pulling off the cover with glee and delight as she emerges. As your infant becomes more mobile, you can vary the game by hiding behind larger obstacles, such as pieces of furniture, and encouraging her to come find you.

- *The Name Game.* Make a game of naming everything around your baby—and don't forget to use her name frequently as well. Parts of the body, letters on alphabet blocks, pieces of furniture, articles of clothing, animals, food, toys and other people make perfect targets for the name game. Involve your baby by asking her to point to things around her which you will then name for her. In time she will probably start "naming" them with you in her own fashion.

- *Books.* Read to your baby every day. Stick with the same book several days in a row and watch her anticipate what is next. Ask her questions about the story and watch for her response. At this age books with one picture per page and large print are best, but from time to time you should read longer stories, too. As you read, point out the objects that are familiar to her. This will help her understand that the story has some relationship to her.

· XV ·

Seven to

Twelve Months

This last stretch of infancy before toddlerhood is a time when individual differences between babies start to become very evident. No two babies have the exact same pattern of development. Yours may concentrate on trying to move across the floor, while another will spend hours practicing her vocal skills. Still another spends most of her time examining the way objects function.

By the end of this period things tend to even out, but some babies focus so intensively on one or two developmental areas that they take a little longer to make their way through the entire list. As long as your baby is absorbed, busy and making progress in a general sense, there's no reason to worry. If your child is lagging behind the neighbor's baby in one area of development, she's probably surging ahead in another.

Here are the major accomplishments you can expect during this period:

Crawling—By the tenth month most babies are active crawlers. The majority start their movement in a backward direction and soon readjust for forward motion, but there are all sorts of variations. Some babies crawl-creep on one side. Others use a backstroke or leapfrog motion. Still others scoot on their bottoms instead of crawling. All methods are perfectly normal. Even if your baby skips crawling entirely and goes directly from creeping to walking, that's normal, too.

Standing—About the same time your baby learns to crawl she may figure out how to bring herself to a standing position, with or without the help of supporting furniture. Once she's discovered the magic of standing, it's only a short time before she discovers how to cruise or walk along the length of a couch or table while holding on with her hands. This is the last stage before fully independent walking.

Sitting Alone—By midway through this period most babies can maneuver themselves into a sitting position and remain upright for long stretches without support. In this position, either in her chair or on the floor, she can eat, play and examine her surroundings. She can also shift from sitting to crawling, so be careful that she is either strapped securely into the high chair or seated in an area where it's safe for her to move around.

Uses Both Hands Independently—By the end of these five months your baby will have almost complete manual dexterity. She'll be able to use each hand independently or both hands together to perform simple tasks. With this new control her hands become tools and, via thumbsucking, sources of comfort.

Social Responses—This is the age of "separation anxiety" when babies typically resist any separation from their mothers or primary caretakers. In some babies this phase lasts only a couple of months, while in others it lasts through most of the second year.

Exploring Spatial Concepts—Your baby is now constantly examining the way things work in relation to herself. By the end of this time she'll be able to find objects that have been hidden from her. She'll understand the difference between near and far, up and down, heavy and light, round and square, and many other basic concepts. The more access she has to objects that illustrate these principles, the more she will experiment and learn.

Babbling—Toward the end of this stage your infant may have a vocabulary of several distinct syllables, including some favorites such as *da da*, *ma ma* or *ba ba*. More important, she probably understands much of what you say to her, particularly common nouns such as the names of familiar people, foods, pets and clothing. The more you continue to talk to her in simple direct language, the more she will comprehend.

Discovery Play during these months must be geared toward your baby's natural interests and enthusiasm. If she seems more absorbed by the challenge of language than by a desire to stand and walk, don't try to redirect her. Pressuring your child to speed up in the areas that interest you may inadvertently slow her down in others. Your baby will show her areas of curiosity and talent. These are bound to be her areas of greatest strength. Bring them out by providing her with tools, encouragement and support without pushing her.

MUSCULAR CONTROL

Both fine and gross motor skills become increasingly refined toward the middle and latter part of this period. These newly acquired skills include squatting, shifting in direction, twisting while sitting and perfecting grasp. Your baby will practice all of these activities tirelessly each and every day. It may not look important to you, but to your baby these seemingly random movements are the means by which she is gaining real control over her life and the world around her. Listed below are a few activities that will help refine her blossoming motor skills.

D I S C O V E R Y   P L A Y

Motor Skills

Here are some games that will help your baby to discover and develop her rapidly emerging motor skills:

- *Feeding Play. Feeding time will become less chaotic as your baby learns to use a spoon for putting food into her mouth as well as making noise. She may even begin to show some hand preferences, right versus left, while eating. You can use mealtimes for Discovery Play by offering her several different kinds of foods that require different levels of skill to handle. Applesauce, yogurt and cereal are great spoon foods, and also nutritious for babies this age.*

- *Ball Play.* Balls make particularly good toys at this time. For variety, use balls of different sizes, colors and textures. They test your infant's ability to coordinate throwing, catching (obviously while sitting on the floor) and hitting. Ball play gives your baby the pleasure of actively participating in a two-way game while also developing her motor abilities.
- *Crawling Over and Behind Obstacles.* If your infant has begun to creep and crawl actively, create games that use and challenge these skills. Place one or two of her favorite toys behind large, soft obstacles, such as cushions, and encourage her to get them. Working her way over and around the obstacles helps her develop strength and coordination while teaching the important lesson that obstacles can be overcome. We want to warn you against making the obstacles too large, or she will simply become frustrated and give up.
- *Follow the Wiggly Line.* A particularly stimulating activity is to "follow the wiggly line." Get your baby's attention and then wiggle a piece of rope or colored string along the ground like a snake in front of her. Infants this age usually can't resist following it if they're beginning to creep. Keep it just out of reach for a brief time, but then let her catch it and manipulate it with her fingers. Change the color or other characteristics of the "snake" if she seems to tire.
- *Catch Me If You Can.* Once she is adept at

crawling around the room, let her chase you. Play these "catch me" games over short distances at first, then expand across the room, into other rooms, behind pieces of furniture and outdoors. Infants this age love these games because they are interactive, involve movement, develop concepts of behind and under, and take them to places they have not been before.

Don't make it too hard in the beginning and don't go far away at first. Your baby may still be in the middle of the phase where she feels separation anxiety. If so, she may get upset if you disappear too abruptly. If you ease her into your disappearances gently, these games can help her adjust to your leaving her for brief times.

• *Pushing and Pulling Games.* As your baby's muscles get stronger she will enjoy flexing and extending them by pushing and pulling things. Start with lighter toys or objects with strings or bars attached that she can push and pull along a smooth surface. After this, you can increase the weight of the toy to increase the challenge. She will probably push more than pull at first, but as she begins to stand, she will love to pull on the string and yank the toy behind her. Change the toys frequently to keep her interested.

• *The Challenge of Stairs.* Your baby's wanderlust personality inevitably will lead her to stairs, which present not only new challenges but potential dangers. Initially, there may be some falling, bumping and bruising as she learns to navigate. Finally, she will realize that, although she can go up the stairs forward, it's probably best to come down backward.

You may be able to save her a few jolts by teaching her in the beginning on a safe "staircase" of her own. Build this play area out of dense foam blocks covered with a soft fabric. This enables her to practice going up and down, getting to a standing position and achieving a better sense of balance.

• *Twirling and Spinning.* Many babies love to have their parents hold them while spinning around in a circle. There is some evidence that this game helps babies sort out the mechanisms they need for balance. Try twirling in one direction, then another, but be careful not to overdo it. Start and stop your spins gently, rotate slowly and maintain the motion only for short periods of time to avoid dizziness.

VISION

From this age until your baby is about three years old, she will spend about 20 percent of her time staring at the world around her. It's not surprising, then, that she is far more attentive to detail than you are. If you change the arrangement of her room even slightly she will notice. If you leave an object behind that was not there before, she probably will race to explore it. Encourage your baby to maintain this concentration by challenging her attention to detail, using the following activities.

DISCOVERY PLAY

Visual Games

- *Looking on the Move. At this age your infant particularly enjoys watching things that move. Take her out often in the stroller or car and help her find active scenes to watch. The zoo, a busy playground, a construction site, the beach and a shopping mall are all ideal places to visit with a young baby. As you look about, point and talk to her about the things she's seeing. She may not understand most of what you're saying, but she'll enjoy the dynamics of the conversation, and she'll look at the things you point out.*
- *Picture Books. During this period, your baby may begin to show a genuine interest in the pictures in books and magazines. Equip her with her own stiff-paged (vinyl pages are ideal) books and let her turn the pages. Talk about the pictures, but don't pressure her to recognize the names of the objects in the pictures or the story line that holds them together. It may take some time yet before she understands the actual concept of a story.*

- *Color Cartons.* Make a game to help bring out your baby's sensitivity to color. Cover three small containers (clean pint-size milk cartons or empty yogurt containers will do) with colored paper. Make two cartons the same color and one different. (The first time you try this, work with highly contrasting colors like blue and yellow. Make later versions of the game with related colors like purple and pink.) Place a small bell, dried beans or other noisemaker in the odd-colored container. With your help your baby will soon learn to identify the noisy carton by its color.

- *Shape Cartons.* Instead of varying the color of the cartons, use cartons of different shapes for this game. Empty, clean oatmeal boxes, plastic jars and cracker boxes work well. Use two boxes and one round container. Cover them with paper of the same color so that they're identical except in shape. Place the noisemaker in the round container. How long does it take your baby to discover that the noise comes from the round container?

- *Package Play.* Some of the best visual aids for your baby are right in your own kitchen. Food packages present your baby with a multitude of colors, shapes, letters, pictures and designs. When empty and clean (we don't advocate giving your baby anything that still contains remnants of food), most are lightweight and safe for your baby to play with. They also challenge *her reaching and grasping skills in a way few store-bought toys do. Here are a few package-toy suggestions that babies we know have liked:*

> *Cans of dehydrated baby food with colored plastic lids*
>
> *Miniature cereal boxes (with the "doors" that open and close)*
>
> *Oatmeal cartons*
>
> *Cookie or cracker boxes*
>
> *Quart-size ice cream containers with lids (well rinsed!)*
>
> *Paper bags from bread loaves*
>
> *Plastic juice bottles*
>
> *Milk cartons*
>
> *Tea or powdered chocolate tins with lids*

LANGUAGE AND SOUNDS

By nine months of age your baby will start using certain sounds meaningfully. Her intonation will become more distinct and you will recognize some specific words, most often "Dada," "Mama," and "Baba." Before the end of her first year she will probably be able to pronounce three to ten words. These are not necessarily words that can be understood by everyone, but they are words nonetheless.

Some babies will know even more words, while others will still be playing around with sound formations.

At times your baby may string series of wordlike sounds together in a gibberish that has all the quality of talk but no real, decipherable words. These combinations of sounds are the beginning of true communication; they have a beginning, an end and a purpose. What's important is for your baby to be making lots of sounds, even if they are nondescript. Sounds of varying intensity, pitch, timbre, and quality are precursors to actual language.

D I S C O V E R Y   P L A Y

Auditory Games

- *Talking.* Conversation remains your baby's best means of learning the fundamentals of language, so talk to her throughout all your activities together. When you are dressing, feeding, bathing and changing her, tell her exactly what you're doing. Be sure you listen to *her* as well. Make conscious efforts to pause and let her babble to you. Then respond to her in an enthusiastic manner.

  If your baby looks away from your face while you are talking, this may be a cue that you are not giving her enough time to respond in her own way. If you find that happening, be quiet and allow her to talk at her own pace.

- *Music.* Just as she must learn about language through listening and practice, she can develop an appreciation of music only by hearing it. Play music often for your baby, at least one to two hours a day. Vary the type of music and watch carefully to see what she seems to like best. Research suggests she will continue to like the music that she heard as a newborn (perhaps even what she heard prenatally), but this is a good time to expose her to new things. The more variety, the merrier. Try music from tapes, records, radio, music boxes and other music-making toys as well as your own singing.

- *Sound Disguises.* If she's like most babies, yours will love to hear you make funny, unnatural sounds. You can do this on your own, or you can use props like a cardboard tube, a kazoo or a paper bag to talk through. When you've finished with the prop hold it for her to talk into. She'll be astonished to hear how different her own voice can sound.

- *Coffee-Can Cling.* Dropping things into an empty coffee can makes delightful sounds. Let your baby try her hand with a can on which you've filed down all the rough edges. Provide her with an assortment of "dropables," like a tennis ball, large beads, spoons, etc. This game *helps bring out her manual dexterity and gives her a lesson in the concept of inside-outside.*

• *Musical Instruments.* Toward the end of this period you can introduce your baby to some real musical instruments. Let her experiment with hollow wood blocks, a xylophone, a triangle (you hold it, she strikes it). If you have a piano, let her try striking some of the keys under your close supervision. If you don't have a piano, you might want to consider buying a toy piano for her to play on her own.

Try to find children's instruments with the musical notes written out on the keys. Although she's still too young to understand the meaning of musical notation, it's a nice idea to establish the connection between the sound and the image as soon as she begins making music.

SMELL, TASTE AND TOUCH

By this age your baby will put everything she touches into her mouth. The messier the project, the more she loves it. While this situation poses some obvious safety hazards, it also provides both of you with the perfect climate for sensory exploration. Your job is to provide your baby with the kinds of substances that are safe for her to taste and explore, but which also provide a challenge to her sensibilities. Here are our suggestions.

D I S C O V E R Y   P L A Y

Touch

- *Water Play.* Beginning at this age small children find liquids of all kinds to be endlessly fascinating. Offer your baby an assortment of waters that have been dyed with food coloring. Let her pour them back and forth, creating new hues as she does. To prevent injuries, always use plastic containers.

  In the summer a wading pool with an inch or two of water, coupled with a collection of containers for pouring, is a full morning's activity. Never leave a baby alone for an instant no matter how shallow the water level is (babies have been known to drown in two or three inches of water). Hoses and sprinklers are equally exciting.

- *Feely Mat.* Bring out your baby's sensitivity to different textures by making a "feely mat" for her to crawl on. Start with an old blanket or large backing cloth. Collect an assortment of textured materials such as velvet, burlap, felt, vinyl, rubber sheeting, nylon mesh, lace, etc. Stitch these materials onto the backing cloth to make a patchwork of textures. To make the cloth even more intriguing, line some of the patches with foam cushioning and turn others into pouches for small toys or rattles. This *gives your baby a great way to entertain herself in the play yard.*

- *Muffin Balls. Another way to introduce your baby to different textures is to fill a muffin tray with different kinds of balls. Tennis balls, rubber balls, pom-poms and plastic eggs will all fit into this holder. Vary the feel, weight and shape of the selection and watch her interest as she explores each one.*

- *Hidden Object Play. Babies can identify objects by feel as accurately as they can by sight. Test this with your baby by allowing her to touch objects she can't see. Either blindfold your baby or hide the objects in a box with a hole cut in it for her hand to enter. After she's had a chance to handle the object, place it alongside an unfamiliar object in front of her. See which she goes toward first. It will probably be the unfamiliar object. This tells you that she recognizes visually the object she has already touched and finds the new one more interesting. As she gets used to this game, try challenging her with objects that are increasingly similar. You'll be astonished at how detailed and discriminating her perceptions are.*

COGNITIVE CHALLENGES

During this period your baby's memory is developing by leaps and bounds. She can now recall events that took place days or even weeks ago and can compare present experiences with them. Her memory is not only more active, but also more accurate, and it takes less stimulation now to trigger a memory from the past.

With her increasing memory she becomes much more finicky about the objects and events that interest her. She'll probably be bored by things that are too familiar, but may avoid things that are totally foreign. Those objects that fall somewhere in the middle are the ones that will capture her attention best. Experiment with your baby to see how far afield you can take her before she loses interest, then keep introducing new experiences that fall within this general range of novelty.

At this age, infants learn a great deal about the characteristics of objects and their relationship to one another. Your baby will be very interested in what happens when objects are dropped, thrown, submerged or placed in containers. She'll experiment with all of these concepts as she solves increasingly complex problems in the course of her play.

This is also the time when your baby learns that objects continue to exist even though they disappear from view (this concept has been termed "object permanence"). She now maintains images of people and objects in her mind even when they are not there and will use these images to look for the originals. When she's about eight months old, your child may be able to find an object that you hide under a blanket, provided she is watching you as you hide it. When she's about ten months old, she might find a hidden object that you move from under one blanket to under another.

This is the age when your child first starts to realize the importance of symbols and labels. She becomes aware of her eyes, ears, nose and mouth, and can find those same body parts on her dolls. She will follow you around the house and imitate what you do, sometimes using objects to act like vacuum cleaners or dust mops. She will act out familiar routines that she has seen or been involved in throughout the day or previous week. These activities mark the beginning of symbolic play.

D I S C O V E R Y   P L A Y

Cognitive Games

- *Hiding Games. Hiding games are an ideal way to help your baby understand the concept of object permanence. These games can take many different forms, for example:*

  1. *"Peekaboo"—Your baby may be losing interest in this game if you've played it a lot before, but you can breathe new life into it by letting her become the active person or hider. Encourage her to "hide" behind a chair or table and pop out for peekaboo. Let her go into the next room and peek around the door. You'll still say "peekaboo," but she will be doing it.*

  2. *"Under Cover"—Hide things under covers as she watches. Keep your eyes focused on your baby as you move the objects around as follows:*

a. Place an object under a cloth in front of her and see if she finds it.

b. Once she can do that reliably, use two cloths. Put the object under one and then, while she is looking, move it under the other cloth. In the early months she will look for the object under the first cloth, even though she saw you move it. With experience she will begin to search for it under the second.

c. Once she has learned how to do this consistently (this may not happen until about ten months or later), try adding a third covering cloth. When she gets good at this, make up your own variations of this game and test her limits. The more she can master, the more fun she will have and the more she will learn about objects and their permanence.

3. *Hiding Things*—With your baby watching, hide an object behind a screen or under a cover, then wait a few moments before letting her retrieve it. See how long she can wait and still find the object. Try progressively more complex sequences. You can even hide yourself. Watch her progress in the problem-solving process as she figures out more and more complicated sequences.

• *Get the Toy.* Fetching games will help your baby discover the relationships between objects while bringing out her problem-solving skills. The idea is to set up two objects so that she must move one in order to retrieve the other. Here are several variations:

1. Set a toy on a scarf or place mat. Position your baby so that the toy is out of reach but the mat is next to her. See how long it takes her to discover that she can get the toy by pulling the mat. What happens if you lift the toy just above the mat or set it so that it's adjacent? Until she understands the concept of "on," she'll continue tugging the mat. Once she's mastered the concept, she'll reach directly for the toy.

2. Place a toy inside a shoe box lying on its side. Does your baby reach for the toy or the whole box? Show her that the toy can be inside or outside the box.

3. Slip a wide ribbon or scarf through a paper tube so it sticks out both ends. Help your baby discover that she can retrieve the scarf by pulling it through the tube.

- *Upside Down and Right Side Up.* At this age your baby is starting to understand the proper orientation of objects in space. Help her explore this concept by turning some of her most familiar belongings upside down from time to time. How does she react when her favorite stuffed animal is perched on his head or her cup is upside down? Try this game with kitchen pots, her infant seat and other household objects. Try it with books and labeled packages to see if she can tell when pictures are upside down.

- *Labeling Objects.* With her love of objects taking firm hold, use your trips outside the house (to the supermarket, Laundromat, drugstore) as opportunities for object identification play. Tell your baby where you are, what's in the grocery cart and what happens to the coins when you're in the Laundromat. Labeling the color, shape, smell, touch and location of the objects you encounter helps to broaden her understanding of her surroundings as well as strengthen her vocabulary.

- *Stacking Play.* Stacking toys and objects help your baby learn about the relative sizes, numbers and quantities of things. Many of these games can be constructed out of things readily available at home (cardboard boxes, towel spools, bobbins). There are also some excellent toys commercially available. Vary the sizes, shapes, colors and textures of the stacking objects as much as possible to hold your infant's interest.

- *Emptying and Filling.* Containers of different shapes and sizes are excellent playthings for your infant. Have her fill them with wooden beads, blocks, toys, water or small objects during playtime, in the bath or at mealtime. This activity promotes fine motor skills and helps her learn about water, gravity, object constancy and cause and effect. The challenge becomes much greater when you use a box or container with a lid that closes, concealing the contents. Talk her through the actions and label the relationships she's creating, such as "empty," "full," "open," "closed," etc. By varying the objects and containers and changing the places where the games are played, you will bring out her sense of curiosity and motivation for mastery.

- *Scribbling and Drawing.* By the end of this period your infant is ready to try her hand at scribbling. Equip her with fat crayons or water-soluble markers and big pads, and let her scribble at random. To help her focus on particular colors and forms, you may want to draw some simple shapes she can try to copy. Don't expect her to succeed, but don't be surprised if her creations are more interesting than your own!

- *Building with Blocks.* Building holds a fascination for infants this age. At first your baby will be able to build a tower of only two or three blocks, but she'll repeat this task again and again until the structures are bigger. Give her large blocks at first that require two hands to hold, then go to smaller blocks, which require finer degrees of motor dexterity. The large letter blocks are especially good at this age because they are easy to manipulate and help familiarize her with the letters of the alphabet.

SOCIAL DEVELOPMENT

Early in this stage you may see new fears emerge, especially of surprises and loud noises (vacuum cleaners are a particular culprit). After months of being easygoing, your baby may now be afraid of bathing or darkness. Try to encourage her to use fantasy play to cope with these upsetting experiences. For example, if vacuum cleaners frighten her, encourage her to play at cleaning the house and imitate the sound of the vacuum cleaner so she can also imitate it. As she plays she'll become more familiar and comfortable with these problem areas. She'll begin to feel that she can control them, and her fears will begin to fade.

As she becomes more capable physically, she also develops a "mind of her own," asserting herself and testing you often. It is approval she is seeking when she comes up to you every few minutes demanding your attention. The best way to handle this is to respond quickly and spontaneously, then encourage her to return to her play. If you're busy with something else, don't ignore her, but explain that she'll have to wait for your full attention. Then *give* her your full attention as soon as possible. Make sure she does not misinterpret your need to attend to other matters as disinterest in her or disapproval of what she is doing.

Now is the time your baby begins to learn the meaning of "no." Sometimes you will even see her shake her head as she is doing something that she knows she should not be doing. Don't be surprised if she becomes sad when told not to do something. The struggle to grasp this concept will carry through into the second year.

Transitional objects (a security blanket, a cherished toy) also become important at this age as infants begin to establish a separate sense of self. The security cloth or blanket gives your baby the reassurance of familiar surroundings as she moves out to explore the world on her own. It functions as an emotional anchor when she is separated from other members of the family. When she is ready, probably around her second birthday, she'll leave it behind. Until that time, let her use it as much as she likes.

Until your baby is eight or nine months old, games are usually controlled and "set up" by you with the baby playing a passive role. Now the roles will begin to reverse as she moves toward independence. Let her steer the direction of things. She'll make it very clear which way she wants to go. Following her lead is the best way for you to bring out her natural assertiveness.

D I S C O V E R Y P L A Y

Self-Expression

Here are just a few of the games you can use to encourage her self-expression:

- *Pat-a-cake. Touch, sound, reaching and social interaction all come together in a good game of pat-a-cake. Consult a Mother Goose book if you've forgotten the rhymes from your own childhood. Modify the game by patting her feet, elbows, knees, cheeks and belly as well as her hands.*

- *Puppet Play.* Puppets give your baby her first taste of fantasy play. These toys needn't be expensive. You can make delightful puppets using old socks, small paper bags, paper plates or old gloves. You can make finger puppets by cutting off the fingers from an old glove and drawing faces on them with markers. Introduce your baby to puppets by manipulating them yourself at first. Give them voices and narrate a story as you move them about. Soon your baby will be ready to control a puppet of her own.

- *Let's Pretend.* Pave the way for your baby's own fantasy play by including her dolls or stuffed animals in your everyday activities. At mealtime let her favorite monkey have a sip of juice or a bite of food along with your baby. At changing time put a diaper on her doll, and at night tuck a stuffed pet in beside her. Incidentally, including her toys in these activities may make it easier for you to introduce her to a new food or a change in the ritual.

- *Dress-ups.* Start a collection of funny clothes for dress play. Sit with your baby in front of a mirror and let her try on different hats, shoes and jewelry. Try some on yourself! Dressing up helps your baby identify the different parts of her body as she begins to establish her own self-image.

As this period draws to a close, it will be hard to believe that your baby is almost one year old. The change by this time, after a predictably slow start, is phenomenal. With her motor and language skills, and her new surge of independence, she is ready to take on the world.

Along with the excitement you will feel because of these changes, there may be a slight sense of loss, a longing for those times when your little one was so dependent and so intimately tied to you. But there is no holding her back. From now on, she is fast becoming her own person.

· XVI ·

Twelve to

Eighteen

Months

Testing is the name of the game now as your baby discovers her own limits. Child psychologist Jean Piaget called these months the Age of Experimentation. No longer content to remain passive, your young toddler now takes an extremely active role in everything that goes on around her. Consumed with the drive to explore and examine her world, she'll insist on doing everything by herself—even tasks that are far beyond her capabilities.

A whirlwind of activity, your baby is truly social now. Though she thinks of herself as separate from you and everyone else in the world, she realizes that she resembles other people in key ways. She's able to understand much of what you say and will soon learn to verbally communicate her most important needs and desires.

She's also beginning to think and question, revealing her intense curiosity and thirst for learning—as well as her willfulness. These developments dominate virtually everything she does during these months, paving the way for many exciting achievements. Here are some of the developmental highlights you can expect:

Locomotion—If your baby is not standing by the end of her first year, she will surely begin to do so, and she'll take her first steps during this period. She may teeter precariously, feet spread wide and legs bent, but in a matter of days she'll start to get the pattern down. With practice comes confidence, so look out! Well before the end of this period she will be running (and falling), climbing and jumping.

Fine Motor Control—In her second year your child will learn to use her hands as expertly as an adult—pinching, gripping and manipulating her fingers at will. She'll spend endless hours practicing these skills on knobs that turn, switches that move, containers that open and close, drawers and doors that pull, and balls that roll and bounce. She'll delight in filling and emptying containers, handling her food and performing countless other manual tasks, which are really games for her.

Problem-solving—Problems, whether they be mental or physical, are the ingredients of learning. At this age your baby will naturally gravitate toward the kinds of problems that help her understand how the objects in her universe operate. She'll experiment with concepts such as "on top," "inside," "in front" and "behind." She'll search for objects that are out of sight, create strategies to obtain objects that are out of reach and experiment with different ways to bring objects under her control.

Fantasy Play—The game of pretend begins as imitation during these months. You'll find her happily "working," "cooking" and "cleaning" just as she's seen you and other members of the family doing. This imaginary play will become more sophisticated as she begins to make up stories to go with her activities. Stuffed and real animals, furniture and ordinary household objects all become props or backdrops for her fantasies.

During these six months the drive to accumulate new information and apply it to action is enormous. Discovery Play capitalizes on your baby's natural motivation by providing lots of learning challenges and opportunities to build on abilities she has developed in the past. Your job as teacher and partner is to provide a responsive environment, guide her into play activities, then stand back and encourage her to make the discoveries that will keep her interest high.

MUSCULAR PLAY

By the end of her first year your baby will be in constant motion. She can now sit down on a chair or bench without looking behind her. She'll pull herself up to a standing position and get down to the floor at will. She can climb up and over tall barriers and bulky pieces of furniture. And her hands are always busy pressing, pulling, pushing and probing everything in sight.

When she first learns to stand your baby will probably want to remain upright at all times, even when being changed or fed. As she learns to walk, however, she may occasionally revert to crawling when she wants to move more rapidly. Every baby takes a slightly different approach to walking. Some sally forth fearlessly, staggering forward until they fall. Others are more reluctant, hanging onto you or a large piece of furniture for safety.

But all babies must take their share of spills and tumbles in the learning process. As distressed as you may feel to see your baby sprawl headlong, try not to let it show to her. She will soon learn to pick herself up and keep going —unless you overreact and make her fearful.

Now that your baby is standing, walking and climbing, there is almost no way to confine her. Rather than making your home a fortress of gates and locked doors, you and your baby will both be much happier if you temporarily reorganize so she can explore freely and safely. Childproofing your home is so crucial to Discovery Play from here on out that we believe it's worth discussing at this point.

Your main objective is to provide an environment that encourages your baby's natural curiosity without compromising her safety. Here are some suggestions:

· Get down on all fours and tour your entire house to see it from your child's perspective. Eliminate dangling cords, breakable objects, sharp corners and small objects that can be easily swallowed.
· Put away breakable furniture or large objects that will easily tip over. Cushion sharp edges and corners of tables and chairs.
· Lock up all medicines in a childproof container out of your baby's reach.
· Keep detergents, cleaning agents, furniture polishes and other chemicals in locked cupboards beyond your child's reach.
· Put safety covers over all sockets. We recommend

putting covers on outlets in use as well as those that are idle. This prevents your baby from pulling plugs out of live sockets.

· Keep all matches out of reach.
· Turn the temperature on your water heater down to 120 degrees so your baby can't accidentally scald herself when in the tub.
· Put a safety latch on drawers or cabinets where knives or other sharp objects are kept.
· Be especially careful when cooking with your toddler underfoot. Keep all handles turned toward the center of the stove and never carry hot liquids when your child is roaming nearby.

Once your home is safe for exploration, help your baby experiment with different ways to explore it. Show her how to climb on and off the sofa, open the door to her closet and go up and down the stairs without harming herself. This exploration will occupy much of her time and allow her to practice her gross motor skills, but she will also welcome activities that help her perfect fine motor skills.

D I S C O V E R Y P L A Y

Motor Skills

These games will help your baby develop her fine and gross motor skills while having fun with you:

- *Ball Play.* Before your baby's first birthday, start collecting balls of different sizes, colors, weights and textures. These will be the most enduring toys in her nursery and offer the most possibilities for games between you. Here are some suggestions:

  —Sit across from your child on the floor and roll two balls of different sizes between you. Show her how they roll at different rates of speed.

  —Play chase, rolling or bouncing a large ball to one side of your baby and encouraging her to go after it and throw or kick it back to you.

  —Give her three fist-sized balls and see if she can figure out how to hold onto all three at once.

  —Give her a "ride" on a large beach ball. Let her sit or lie on top of it as you gently roll her back and forth. Tell her which direction she's moving as you push her "right," "left," "forward," "back."

- *Tunnel Crawl.* Make tunnels out of couch pillows or large empty boxes and show your baby how to wiggle through. Reward her with a happy shout of surprise when she emerges from the end. This activity will help her refine her crawling skills as it teaches her the concepts of inside and outside.

- *Ride a Towel.* Seat or lay your baby on the end of a towel and pull her around the house. Early

in her second year she'll have a hard time staying on, so start slowly. With time and practice
she'll learn to hang on and you can pick up the
speed.

• *Cleaning House.* Make a game for your baby
out of your own chores. Let her push the vacuum cleaner for you. Show her how to push in
the chairs around the dining room table. Let
her help you make the beds or wipe the coun-
tertops. These activities will help her stretch
her muscles and also give her a feeling of importance as she works by your side.

• *Take Out and Put Back.* Set up floor-level
shelves or drawers around the house with toys,
books or unbreakable objects that your baby
can take down and put back. Ask her to go to
"her shelf" and bring you a specific object. By
responding to your request, she'll be applying
her new language and cognitive skills as well as
her motor abilities.

• *Pushing and Pulling.* Even after she learns to
walk securely your baby will love the feeling of
control that pushing and pulling large toys
gives her. Most babies delight in the toys that
make noises, waddle or pop up and down as
they move down the street. Carriages, wagons
and toy shopping carts are equally fun and encourage fantasy play as well.

• *Scooters.* Toward the end of this period your
baby is ready to try a low three-wheel scooter.
Show her how to push herself across the play-

ground or backyard, but make sure she stays away from driveways and street traffic.

· *Tools, Workbenches and Pegboards (with large pegs that she can't possibly swallow). Although you may think your baby uses these only to make noise, they also help her improve her hand-eye coordination and encourage fantasy play. Workbenches with individual slots for tools of different shapes present her with a cognitive challenge as well.*

· *Park Play. By now your baby is ready to have a good workout on the <u>toddler play equipment</u> at the local park. Well before the end of these six months she'll master the slide, seesaw and*

swings. Here are some other playground activities that are especially beneficial for her developing motor skills:

—*Monkey Bar Hang.* Hold your baby up to one rung of the monkey bars and let her wrap her hands around it. Once she's got a good grip, let her hang (keeping your hands at the ready to catch her if she falls). Gradually work up to a count of ten. You can also do this at home, lifting her just an inch or two off the floor as she hangs from a wooden dowel that you hold over her head.
—*Climbing the Slide.* Coming down a slide is easy, but climbing up it requires much more coordination. Help your baby learn to use her hands and feet to climb up the ramp as well as the ladder.
—*Balance Beam.* If your park has a low balance beam, by all means let your baby use it. The beam is a wonderful way for her to improve her eye-foot coordination, poise and balance in walking. Place a favorite toy at one end of the beam and start her at the other. You'll need to hold both her hands at first. By the end of this period she may be able to walk the beam unassisted.

VISION PLAY

At this age your baby's vision is probably better than yours, but she is still learning how to observe things correctly. Many children never learn to focus their full attention when looking about. Instead, their glance flits briefly here and there without ever seeing in detail. This pattern eventually becomes a habit and can be a serious handicap to later education.

You can build your baby's skills of observation by providing visual games that require her to look carefully at the fine details of objects, shapes and colors. Here are some suggestions.

D I S C O V E R Y   P L A Y

Visual Acuity

- *Jigsaw Puzzles:* Puzzles help children focus on several elements at once: the shape of each individual puzzle piece, the fine detail of the picture on each piece and the position of each piece within the puzzle as a whole. Start with puzzles consisting of three or four large pieces depicting animals, houses or other familiar images. You can easily make your own by pasting a large photograph or picture from a magazine onto a sheet of cardboard and cutting it into several large shapes. Gradually progress to puzzles with more and smaller pieces.
- *Matching Games.* Finding identical pairs in an assortment of similar objects is another way your child can develop her sensitivity to detail.

You can play this game using playing cards, letter blocks, balls or spools on which you've painted colors or patterns.

Start with a set of two pairs of objects that are distinctly different from each other. Spread the pieces randomly in front of your baby and show her how to match them up. As she gets used to the game, present her with a larger selection of pairs and make the differences more subtle. As the game gets more complex, she'll learn to concentrate more closely on the fine details.

• *Form Boards and Shape Sorters.* These toys, which will continue to challenge your baby throughout her second year, develop her visual concentration, tactile sensitivity and cognitive perception.

They also introduce her to the basic geometric forms that are so important in reading, writing and mathematics. Shape sorters come in a wide variety of shapes and forms, from balls and boxes to little toy houses and clowns, into which she fits blocks of different shapes. Form boards are flat, like jigsaw puzzles, with cutout forms which she can put in and take out. It's easy for babies to become frustrated by this game if there are too many pieces, so start with a very simple model.

• *Changing Dimensions.* Cut pictures of familiar objects out of old magazines, then collect the corresponding real objects, matching the pictures as exactly as possible (for example, a picture of an orange and a real orange). Lay the objects and pictures out in a group in front of your child and ask her to "put the oranges together," "put the books together," and so forth. This may be a difficult game at first, so help your child, and if she gets too frustrated, stop and try another day.

- *Crayons and Fingerpaints.* Now is the time to give your baby a set of her own fat crayons, fingerpaints and a large pad of paper to fill with color. Watch how she uses her whole arm to make sweeping strokes. Encourage her to experiment with different color combinations. You may also want to try some of the finger-paint soaps that can be used in the tub.

HEARING

Your baby's appreciation for music, rhythm and sounds associated with objects and activity continues to expand during this period. The following discovery activities will help you explore the world of sound together.

D I S C O V E R Y   P L A Y

Hearing

- *Noise Labels.* Name the sounds in your child's world just as you do animals, objects and people she sees. If she startles at the sound of a

siren, tell her, *"That's the sound of a fire en-gine."* If you hear chirping overhead, tell her, *"That's a bird chirping."* If the sound source is visible, point it out to her and show her how the sound is made: *"The wheels are squeaking as they turn."*
- *Musical Concepts.* As your child plays her toy piano or xylophone, describe some of the tunes she's composing in basic musical terms. Show her the difference between high and low notes, for example. Show her how to play fast or slow. Demonstrate different kinds of rhythms and let her create her own.

SMELL, TASTE AND TOUCH

Now that your baby is actively "into everything" you may have to remind yourself that touching and tasting are vital forms of exploration for her. You naturally will hold her back from exploring dangerous substances and surfaces too closely, but don't restrict her more than you have to. Look for safe activities you can do together that will satisfy her need to smell, taste and touch.

D I S C O V E R Y P L A Y

Smell, Taste and Touch

- *Collages.* You'll have to do the actual construc-tion of the collage, but let your child select and arrange the components. Pull from as many different sources as you can in order to stimulate all your baby's senses. Here are some suggestions:

> Leaves and flowers (make sure they're nontoxic)
> Magazine clippings
> Cutouts from food packages
> Scraps of fabric and foil
> Small, dry foods (cereal, dry pasta and rice, etc.)
> String and ribbon
> Wood, stone, shells
> Nontoxic paints, crayons, markers

• *The Kitchen Laboratory. Give your baby a chance to play master chef every now and then. Equip her with a selection of foods with different colors and textures, and a large bowl and spoon with which to mix them. She'll make a mess, so be prepared for a major cleanup afterward (of the kitchen and her). She'll have such fun it's worth the inconvenience. Make sure the foods she uses are safe for her to taste and keep the portions small so she doesn't waste too much. Here are some suggestions for your young chef:*

> water or soda water
> cottage cheese
> fruit yogurt
> crumbled cracker or cookie

> *applesauce*
> *cranberry or cherry juice (for color)*
> *ready-to-eat cereal*
> *cut-up fruit*

- *Sticky Stuff. Let your baby experiment with sticky textures. Provide her with an assortment of stickers, labels, household tape, cloth adhesives and bandages. Ask her to put one kind of sticker on her hand, another on her knee, and so on. This is a great way to help her learn the names of her body parts.*

COGNITIVE CHALLENGES

The most astounding cognitive development during this period is the emergence of language. All those early months of pointing, labeling, reading and explaining are now paying off. Your baby understands much of what you say and can even say a few words herself. By about fourteen months most babies understand the following words and phrases:

water	drink
ears	eyes
book	get up
socks	cup
bring	hair
brush your hair	hi/hello
stand up	dog/doggy
car	kitty/cat

chair/highchair	pat-a-cake
come here	peekaboo
sit up	cracker

By about eighteen months your baby may also understand:

apple	milk
teeth	bed
show me	don't touch
blanket	coat/sweater
cereal	bottle
spoon	open/close the door

Not only does she learn specific words during this period, but she also starts to understand the inflections of normal speech, such as the way you raise your voice at the end of a sentence to indicate a question or drop your voice to end a definitive statement. She now realizes that a soft, quiet tone means that all is well, while a loud, abrupt voice means that something is wrong or urgent. The *way* you talk to your baby is as important as the words you use.

By her first birthday your baby may be able to say as many as six words like "mama," "dada," "papa," "hi," "bye-bye"—mostly short words beginning with *b, p* or *m,* which are the easiest consonants to pronounce. You'll also find her babbling words that sound nonsensical to you, but listen closely and you'll hear the rhythms and inflections of real language. By the end of this period she'll apply the same vocal patterns to mini-sentences of words that you can understand.

Her new verbal skills are the most stunning, but by no means her only cognitive achievements during this period. According to one study, babies this age spend about 20 to 40 percent of their time experimenting with small objects, about twice as much time as they spend socializing with other people.

During these play periods your baby will learn many critical concepts about spatial relationships, such as "on," "inside," "on top," "in front," "outside," "behind." She'll learn now about shapes of objects, and she'll discover, for example, that a round block fits in a round hole but not a square one. She'll also discover many of the principles of quantity and one-to-one matching that form the basis of mathematics.

The best way for you to help her discover these relationships between objects and concepts is to present her with focused problems and help her develop solutions.

DISCOVERY PLAY

Cognitive Challenges

- *Nesting Bowls and Containers.* Present your baby with five or six containers that are identical in every way but size. What does she do with them? At this age she'll probably experiment with fitting them into each other. In time she'll realize there is a specific order to these objects, from largest to smallest, and that they all will fit *inside of* each other if she follows this order. You'll find many different kinds of toys that can teach her this principle, from nesting blocks to dolls. You can also use a set of plastic mixing bowls or measuring cups. Help your child by laying the set in front of her in a line from smallest to largest, then show her how they nest.

• *Tower Building.* Show your child how to turn her nesting blocks over and stack them to build a tower. This game will help her learn what relative size means when you're putting objects *on top of* each other. Start with just two or three large blocks and gradually present her with smaller blocks as her manual dexterity improves. She'll have as much fun knocking the tower down as building it, but it's all part of the learning process.

• *Nuts and Bolts.* Give your baby a set of large plastic nuts and bolts (making sure the pieces are too large to swallow). Help her discover how to take one pair apart and put it together; then take all the pairs apart, mix up the pieces and ask her to put them together again. At first she'll try to put very big nuts on very small bolts, and vice versa, but with your help she'll learn to sort the pieces by size before putting the pairs together. Don't do *all* the work for her or you'll lose the value and the fun of this play activity.

• *Hiding Games.* Help your baby learn the concepts of "in front," "on top," "next to," "behind" and "under" by moving a toy to the various positions around a large box. Tell her where the toy is—"in front of the box"—and ask her to get it. To make the game more challenging, use two or three boxes as hiding places and move the toy from one to another. Ask her, "Which box is the toy under?" Early in her second year she may have to search under all the boxes even if she watched you move the toy. Later she will be able to track and remember your actions.

- *Catching and Retrieving.* At this age, when your child sees an attractive toy that's out of reach, she'll work hard to come up with a solution to the problem. When she succeeds, she feels tremendously powerful and proud of herself.

  Challenge her by tying a string to one of her favorite toys and positioning her so that she's within reach of the string but not the toy. See if she understands that pulling the string will move the toy. If she doesn't pull the string on her own, show her how to do it. The next day tie the string to a different toy and see if she remembers what to do. If she doesn't, show her again but don't push her. This is a difficult but important concept for her to learn. You can try many different variations of this game using sticks, small strainers or other tools to retrieve the object. In the tub give your baby a small strainer and show her how to catch her floating toys.

- *Body Parts.* Your toddler is fascinated with the parts of her body. Help her learn their names by singing and pointing to each one on her body and on yours. Move her arms and legs, kick her feet, play peekaboo with her eyes and kiss her cheeks to provide extra emphasis as you sing the names. Then let her watch as your repeat the song pointing to the same body parts on yourself. Soon, when you ask, "Where's your nose?" or "Where's mommy's nose?" she'll be able to answer by pointing. This process helps her discover that she is a person just like you, but separate.

· *Opposites.* These games allow your baby to experience the contrast between the opposite concepts as you label them for her. Here are some suggestions:

—Swing your baby in your arms "Up high!" and "Down low!"
—Take your baby's hands and move her arms "Out" and "In," "Up" and "Down." Do the same with her legs.
—Let her flip the light switch so the room is "Light" and "Dark."
—Let her roll a small ball "Into" and "Out of" a box or can.

· *Reading Aloud.* Reading continues to be one of the most important activities you can do with your baby. Now that she can understand more words she'll be even more interested in stories than she was before. She'll also be receptive to other information about the book, such as the title and format.

As you look at a book together tell her the title and author. Talk about the cover, illustrations and the number of pages. Run your finger under the text as you read to show her how writing begins at the upper left corner and moves toward the right and down the page. All of these motions help familiarize your baby with the form and purpose of the printed word.

SOCIAL DEVELOPMENT

By the end of her first year your baby has learned a great deal about the people she lives with. She knows that adults can ease her discomfort and increase her pleasure, and she's discovered how to call or cry for them to come when she needs them. Now she's ready to fine-tune these requests for help so that she can use adults as a learning resource as well as emergency aid.

Early in her second year she'll begin to express her emotions more clearly to adults. Watch carefully and you'll see a much broader range of feelings than she showed before. There are subtle differences between similar emotions, like glee, amusement, contentment and delight. Your baby is starting to recognize these differences, and she's also learning to direct her emotion. Instead of the general rage she used to feel when she was hurt or frustrated, she may now direct her anger at you. By the same token, she'll dole out her affection more consciously than she did in the past.

By far the most exciting emotion to surface at this age is the pride she takes in her accomplishments. As she crawls, walks, stands and climbs about the house she'll frequently check back to see your reaction. She knows when she does something marvelous and anticipates your praise. As you applaud her she'll beam with excitement and pride. Your responses help motivate her to pursue these feats of discovery.

Your life would be a lot easier if she *only* did things you approve of. Unfortunately, at this age your baby is determined to do things her own way even if it means a clash of wills with you. Discipline is now a necessity. If you maintain clear, reasonable limits your child will soon learn to accept that she can't always have her own way. The key word here is *maintain*.

Toddlers are only good listeners when they want to be, and they never want to hear the word "no." When your child is doing something forbidden, you'll probably have to stop her several times before she accepts the restriction. Gently but firmly guide her into a different activity and praise her each time she remembers the rule on her own. This takes a lot of persistence (and patience) on your part, but eventually your baby will realize that you mean what you say. You'll have an easier time than less consistent parents whose children soon learn to wait out the restrictions.

By setting sensible limits and providing encouragement for positive behavior, you help your baby develop a balanced view of her place among other people. She realizes that she can affect the way other people feel about her, and that they can affect the way she feels about herself.

She discovers that she is a special person, but not at the expense of another person's rights. The following activities will help reinforce these discoveries.

D I S C O V E R Y   P L A Y

Social Interaction

- *Personal Habits.* The best way for your child to learn to take care of herself physically is by watching you. Getting dressed, brushing your teeth and hair, and washing your face can all become important discovery games if you involve your baby. Let her watch you and show her how to do these things herself. Turn them into a daily ritual for her just as they are for you. In addition to teaching her the basics of good grooming, you'll be arming her with experiences she can draw on for fantasy play.

- *Mirror Faces.* Your toddler is likely to be just as fascinated with mirrors now as she was in her infancy. The difference is that she is discovering the difference between herself and her reflection.

  To help reinforce this discovery, subtly "paint" her face when she's not looking, then see how she responds to her mirror image. A daub of lipstick on her nose or cheek will catch her attention. If she reaches up to rub the color off her own nose, she understands what a reflection is. Then she's ready for you to paint her face in earnest, using makeup or face paint. Let her watch in the mirror as you apply the paint, then have her trace the lines herself using the reflection as her guide.

• *Mine and Yours.* With her increasing awareness of herself as an individual, she now realizes the difference between "mine" and "yours" and will delight in trading objects back and forth with you to demonstrate this difference. Start the game yourself by giving her one of her toys and asking, "Is that mine or yours?" She may point to herself, hug the toy tighter or give it back to you by way of response. Try the game with objects that she identifies with you (a piece of your clothing, your hairbrush, your key ring) and see if her answer changes.

• *Doll Play.* Both boys and girls benefit tremendously from dolls at this age. Through these pretend friends your child can practice different ways to behave toward other people. She can feed, bathe and dress her doll to see what it feels like to be Mommy in these situations. At the store she can introduce her doll to the people she meets there. Throughout the day she can practice being a friend to her doll even when no other children are around. All of these activities will enhance your child's confidence in real-life social situations.

- *Telephone.* Playing telephone is a fantasy game that helps your child develop a valuable social skill. Letting her play with real phones can be dangerous (to the phone and your phone bill), so equip her with a toy phone of her own. Show her how to dial, answer the phone and say good-bye. Read off the numbers as she dials them so that she mentally starts to connect her action with the number. Let her join you on some real phone calls. She'll delight in hearing a real voice at the other end of the line, but don't expect her to say much herself. Once she discovers the joys of a real phone, keep the instrument well out of her reach or your phone bill could skyrocket.
- *Social Graces.* This is the time for your child to discover the power she can wield over adults by using everyday social graces. Show her how to shake hands, wave bye-bye, applaud and hold the door for other people. People will be charmed and delighted to see her perform these grownup courtesies, and their responses will help her turn these into long-lasting habits.

Moving into the next phase of your baby's life is like crossing a bridge over which you know you'll never return. There's a clear separation between you now. You are no longer the only influence on her development as she reaches out toward other people and sources of information in the world outside.

Many parents view this new independence with some ambivalence, if not outright sadness. It's not easy to say good-bye to the enchanting baby you greeted just eighteen months ago. But think how exciting it will be to help her through the rest of her childhood! Don't try to hold her back. Instead, step back and gently urge her off. Lengthen the string of attachment between you and enjoy the delightfully special person she is and will be.

Epilogue

For the rest of her life, your child will continue to be special, and her success and happiness will continue to depend—at least in part—on the recognition and development of her unique interests and abilities. So, while specific activities may change as your child passes from infancy to toddlerhood, and then on through childhood and adolescence to adulthood, the underlying principles and process that determine your relationship with her should not. The games may change, but your Discovery Play together should go on.

As much as ever before, your child needs an environment that nurtures her interests, encourages her explorations and supports her development in directions that are meaningful to her. It is the framework within which she will build her self-image. It is the foundation on which she will build self-esteem.

As much as you can, for the rest of her life, create that environment for your child. It is the key to a lifetime of happiness and health. It is the greatest gift any parent can give a child.

The
Discovery
Diary

Bringing out the best in your baby depends upon your discovering those characteristics that make her unique. Recognition of her range of abilities at each stage of growth is one important element. Identification of her particular likes and dislikes is equally important.

The way to discover her special self is through your observations of her and your interactions with her. At the same time, she learns about you. The process of discovery helps bring you and your baby closer together.

The Discovery Diary is provided as a tool for your use in this process. You can use it to record the milestones in your baby's development, her personal preferences and your other observations about her during the first eighteen months.

HOW TO USE THE DISCOVERY DIARY

In the MILESTONES sections, check off each new development under the month in which it occurs. To keep a more detailed record, write in the actual date instead of a check. Be alert to the sequence of developments and keep in mind your baby's current repertoire of abilities as you interact with her.

In the PREFERENCES sections, describe your baby's favorites in the spaces provided. If there are some favorites you can't tell, make a note of that fact instead. Notice how her preferences change or stay the same from month to month. Compare them with your own.

In the OTHER OBSERVATIONS sections, write in any other particulars you notice about your baby's personality, abilities, responses and interactions with you. Note anything at all that comes to your attention. Watch for themes or special qualities to come into focus. This is a good place to keep track of language development and relationships with other people and to describe her fantasy play.

Remember, this is neither a test nor a race, and there are no right or wrong answers. The purpose of this diary is simply to help you get to know your baby better and to help you deliver the gift of self-esteem.

DISCOVERY DIARY
Birth Through Three Months

	Month 1	Month 2	Month 3
MILESTONES Roots when you stroke cheek			
Steps when upright			
"Swims" on stomach			
Begins to smile			
Focuses ten to twelve inches			
Focuses up to one yard			
Focuses across room			
Tracks moving objects			
Avoids approaching objects			
Startles at sudden noise			
Turns toward sounds			
Responds to your voice			
Babbles and coos			
Laughs			
Shows interest in mirrors			
Recognizes familiar objects			

DISCOVERY DIARY
Birth Through Three Months (cont.)

	Month 1	Month 2	Month 3
Learns to control mobile			
Sucks hands and fingers			
Watches hands and fingers			
Bats at objects			
Kicks at objects or target			
Supports own head			
Sits with support			
PREFERENCES Favorite scents:			
Favorite textures:			
Favorite colors:			
Favorite patterns:			
Favorite sounds:			
Favorite music:			
Favorite toys:			
Favorite books:			
Favorite places:			

OTHER OBSERVATIONS

DISCOVERY DIARY
Four Through Six Months

	Month 4	Month 5	Month 6
MILESTONES Sucks hands			
Sucks toes			
Reaches for objects and people			
Kicks objects/targets			
Grasps objects with one hand			
Grasps objects with two hands			
Pinches objects with fingers			
Brings objects to mouth			
Transfers objects hand to hand			
Plays with rattle			
Handles three toys at a time			
Recognizes mother			
Recognizes father			
Recognizes brother/sister/ grandparent			
Recognizes sitter			

DISCOVERY DIARY
Four Through Six Months (cont.)

	Month 4	Month 5	Month 6
Interested in other babies			
Balks at strangers			
Plays peekaboo			
Babbles at mirror			
Imitates facial expressions			
Watches things upside down			
Looks for hidden objects			
Shows anger			
Recognizes own name			
Rolls over front to back			
Rolls over back to front (May not occur until after sixth month)			
Creeps forward/backward (May not occur until after sixth month)			
Sits up (May not occur until after sixth month)			

	Month 4	Month 5	Month 6
PREFERENCES Favorite tastes:			
Favorite scents:			
Favorite textures:			
Favorite colors:			
Favorite patterns:			
Favorite sounds:			
Favorite music:			
Favorite toys:			
Favorite books:			
Favorite places:			

OTHER OBSERVATIONS

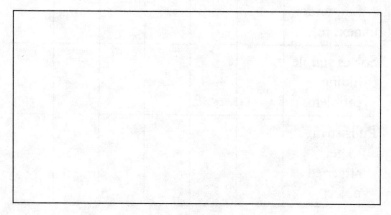

269

DISCOVERY DIARY
Seven Through Twelve Months

	Month 7	Month 8	Month 9	Month 10	Month 11	Month 12
MILESTONES Remembers objects						
Shows separation anxiety						
Shows fear						
Shows shyness						
Shows sadness						
Shows guilt						
Understands spatial relationships: (on, under, next to)						
Solves simple hiding problems						
Pulls string to get attached object						

	Month 7	Month 8	Month 9	Month 10	Month 11	Month 12
Squeezes toy to make squeak						
Interested in water						
Fills and empties containers						
Drinks from a cup						
Says first words						
Imitates sounds						
Understands words						
Understands "No"						
Uses fantasy play						

DISCOVERY DIARY
Seven Through Twelve Months (cont.)

	Month 7	Month 8	Month 9	Month 10	Month 11	Month 12
Rolls over both ways						
Crawls						
Climbs stairs						
Pulls self to sit						
Pulls self to stand						
Bounces when standing						
Sits down from standing position						
Stands alone (May not occur until after twelfth month)						
Walks with help						

	Month 7	Month 8	Month 9	Month 10	Month 11	Month 12
Walks alone (May not occur until after twelfth month)						
Uses hands independently						
Claps						
Waves good-bye						
Bangs objects together						
Feeds self						
Reaches to be picked up						
Rolls a ball						
Stacks two to three blocks						
Uses push toy						
Uses pull toy						

DISCOVERY DIARY
Seven Through Twelve Months (cont.)

	Month 7	Month 8	Month 9	Month 10	Month 11	Month 12
PREFERENCES Favorite tastes:						
Favorite scents:						
Favorite textures:						
Favorite colors:						
Favorite patterns:						
Favorite sounds:						
Favorite music:						
Favorite toys:						
Favorite books:						

	Month 7	Month 8	Month 9	Month 10	Month 11	Month 12
Favorite places:						
OTHER OBSER-VATIONS First words						
New words						
Knows names						

DISCOVERY DIARY
Thirteen Through Eighteen Months

	Month 13	Month 14	Month 15	Month 16	Month 17	Month 18
MILESTONES Understands big/small						
Walks alone						
Walks up and down stairs						
Runs						
Jumps in place						
Kicks ball						
Throws ball						
Scribbles						
Stacks three to six blocks						
Turns knobs/ switches						
Sorts shapes						
Solves simple puzzles						

DISCOVERY DIARY
Thirteen Through Eighteen Months (cont.)

	Month 13	Month 14	Month 15	Month 16	Month 17	Month 18
Uses pegboard						
Uses spoon						
Drinks from cup						
Follows simple directions						
Recognizes sounds						
Names objects						
Makes two-word sentences						
Sings						
Turns pages of book						
Puts toys away						

	Month 13	Month 14	Month 15	Month 16	Month 17	Month 18
Points to body parts						
Says "mine"						
Shows separation anxiety						
Uses fantasy play						
Remembers where objects are hidden						
PREFERENCES Favorite tastes:						
Favorite scents:						
Favorite textures:						

DISCOVERY DIARY
Thirteen Through Eighteen Months (cont.)

	Month 13	Month 14	Month 15	Month 16	Month 17	Month 18
Favorite colors:						
Favorite patterns:						
Favorite sounds:						
Favorite music:						
Favorite toys:						
Favorite books:						
Favorite places:						

OTHER OBSERVATIONS

Bibliography

Bank Street College of Education, *Raising a Confident Child*. New York: Pantheon Books, 1984.

Bloom, Benjamin S., *Developing Talent in Young People*. New York: Ballantine Books, 1985.

Bower, T. G. R., *A Primer of Infant Development*. San Francisco: W. H. Freeman & Co., 1977.

Brazelton, T. Berry, *Infants and Mothers*. New York: Dell Publishing Co., 1983.

Bruner, Jerome S., *Child's Talk: Learning to Use Language*. New York: W. W. Norton & Co., 1983.

Caplan, Frank, *The First Twelve Months of Life*. New York: Bantam Books, 1980.

Caplan, Frank and Theresa, *The Second Twelve Months of Life*. New York: Bantam Books, 1980.

Crain, William C., *Theories of Development: Concepts and Applications*. Englewood Cliffs, N.J.: Prentice-Hall, Inc., 1980.

Fraiberg, Selma H., *The Magic Years*. New York: Scribner's, 1959.

Gooch, Nancy, and Sexton, David, *How to Maximize Your Child's Potential*. New York: Cornerstone Library, 1984.

Grasselli, Rose, and Hegner, Priscilla, *Playful Parenting*. New York: Putnam Publishing Group, 1981.

Hagstrom, Julie, *More Games Babies Play*. New York: A&W Publishers, Inc., 1981.

Haith, Marshall, *Rules That Babies Look By*. Hillsdale, New Jersey: Lawrence Earlbaum Assoc., 1980.

Jackson, Jane Flannery and Joseph H., *Infant Culture*. New York: Thomas Y. Crowell, Publishers, 1978.

Kagan, Jerome, *The Nature of the Child.* New York: Basic Books, Inc., 1984.

Kagan, Jerome, Kearsley, Richard, and Zelazo, Philip, *Infancy: Its Place in Human Development.* Cambridge, Mass.: Harvard University Press, 1980.

Klaus, Marshall H., and Kennell, John H., *Maternal-Infant Bonding.* Saint Louis, Mo.: C. V. Mosby Co., 1976.

Leach, Penelope, *Your Baby & Child: From Birth to Age Five.* New York: Alfred A. Knopf, 1985.

Mahler, Margaret, Pine, Fred, and Bergman, Anni, *The Psychological Birth of the Human Infant.* New York: Basic Books, 1975.

Oppenheim, Joanne S., *Kids and Play.* New York: Ballantine Books, 1984.

Princeton Center for Infancy, *The Parenting Advisor.* New York: Doubleday, 1977.

Segal, Marilyn, *Birth to One Year.* White Plains, N.Y.: Mailman Press, 1983.

Singer, Dorothy G. and Jerome L. *Partners in Play: A Step-by-Step Guide to Imaginative Play in Children.* New York: Harper & Row, 1977.

Singer, Dorothy G., and Revenson, Tracey A. *A Piaget Primer: How a Child Thinks.* New York: New American Library, 1978.

Stern, Daniel, *The First Relationship: Infant and Mother.* Cambridge, Mass.: Harvard University Press, 1977.

——— *The Interpersonal World of the Infant.* New York: Basic Books, 1985.

Treleasy, Jim, *The Read-Aloud Handbook.* New York: Penguin Books, 1985.

Tronick, Edward, and Adamson, Lauren, *Baby As People.* New York: Collier Books, 1980.

Weissbourd, Bernice, and Musick, Judith, *Infants: Their Social Environments.* Washington, D.C.: National Association for the Education of Young Children, 1981.

White, Burton L., *The First Three Years of Life.* Englewood Cliffs, N.J.: Prentice-Hall, Inc., 1975.

Willemsen, Eleanor, *Understanding Infancy.* San Francisco: W. H. Freeman & Co., 1979.

Index

Physical abnormality, and speech
problems, 131, 133
Physical development, and
emotional security, 144
Picture books, 214
Pincer grasp, 187
Plate faces, 173, 194
See also Human face
Play, 8, 11, 23
Playground equipment, 239–40
Poems, 128, 178
Position changes, 101
Positive reinforcement, 17
Predictability of parental
behavior, 31
Premature babies, 6, 82–83
Pressure for achievement, and
stuttering, 133
Problem solving, 114–15
four to seven months, 203–4
seven to twelve months, 224,
225
twelve to eighteen months,
233
Protectiveness, and separation
anxiety, 149
Pull toys, 106, 212, 238
Puppet play, 230
Pushing off, 190
Push-pull play. *See* Pull toys
Puzzles, 109, 241

Quantity concepts, 123–25, 226
twelve to eighteen months,
248

Rattles, 179, 197
Reaching, 97–100
four to seven months, 187,
188

Reading to infant, 127–29
birth to four months, 184–85
four to seven months, 196,
206
twelve to eighteen months,
251–52
Recordings of family voices, 180
Recreation, and intellectual
development, 8
Reflexes, 35–36, 159–61, 164
Reinforcement, 17
in language development, 60
Respect, parent-child, 15–16
Responsive environment, 13–14,
27
Retrieval games, 250
Rhythmic sounds, 180–81
cross-modal matching, 46
verse, 178
Ribbon fan, 169–70
Rocking chairs, 110
Rocking of baby, 162, 163
Roles, in learning, 24–26
Rolling over, 102, 188, 189
Roly-poly toys, 193–94
Rooting reflex, 35, 161
Rote learning, by superbabies,
5
Routine, 29, 30, 31
Rovee-Collier, Carolyn, 49–52

Safety of environment, 28,
235–36
Scent books, 199
Scientists, early education, 8, 9
Scooters, 238–39
Screens, hiding games, 224
Scribbling, 227
Search games, 204, 221, 212,
249–50

292